Male Eating Disorders

Russell Delderfield

Male Eating Disorders

Experiences of Food, Body and Self

palgrave
macmillan

Russell Delderfield
University of Bradford
Bradford, UK

ISBN 978-3-030-02534-2 ISBN 978-3-030-02535-9 (eBook)
https://doi.org/10.1007/978-3-030-02535-9

Library of Congress Control Number: 2018963229

This Palgrave Pivot imprint is published by the registered company Springer Nature Switzerland AG
The registered company address is: Gewerbestrasse 11, 6330 Cham, Switzerland

For my Mam and Dad, Val and Keith, and my brother, Roly, who love me whether I am fat or thin, mad or sane, struggling or recovering.

For Ian and Gillian, who know exactly why they are mentioned here.

For any man who experiences disordered eating.

You are not alone.

Preface

This book began life as my doctoral project that I undertook part-time whilst working, until last year. The text is the result of extensive scholarly endeavour in making sense of men's experiences of eating disorder, using interpretative analysis of primary data. This is something that is woefully under-represented in our field, despite the lives that disordered eating affects. In addition, the work embraces a reflexive approach, as I have personal experience of being a man with an eating disorder.

I have had more than one career before finally realising my dream of doing research, I have no doubt that these other life experiences have contributed to the eclectic and trans-disciplinary foundation that has informed my thinking about male experience. The social psychology represented here has been fed by diverse ideas from within and without psychology. My hope is that this will allow readers access to a broader base of understanding about this phenomenon.

In the main text, I rely on an elementary understanding of the main eating disorders, as these have not been described using their clinical criteria. Forgive me if this hinders immediate engagement with the book. I thoroughly recommend *Beat Eating Disorders* website for highly-accessible lay descriptions of the main disorders.

This leads me to a brief note about terminology. As will be seen, I have not insisted on formal clinical diagnoses from the men who have contributed. I use eating disorder and disordered eating interchangeably with no pretensions to recognised clinical definitions. I perceive the words 'male' and 'female', used as nouns, to be the province of medicalised, biological terms for sex. On occasion, for clarity, I have needed to adopt this nominal use. Otherwise, my main uses are adjectival, as demonstrated by the book's title. Wherever possible I have used men/boys and women/girls, as these denote socially constructed gender, as well as being common parlance. 'He' and related pronouns feature heavily. I make no apology for this as I am foregrounding the lives of men. Other pronouns that appear, that may be troubling to some readers, are 'I' and 'we'. Above, and in greater detail in Chap. 1, I make it clear that I am implicated in the interpretative work that I have undertaken, therefore, I need to own this where appropriate. On occasion, I have made judicious use of 'we' where I need to be clear that I am referring to the four stories featured together with myself.

Lastly, a mild word of warning. I believe in books because they can be accessed and read by anybody. 'Anybody' means that someone may read this who has intimate knowledge of living with an eating disorder. I have not stinted on the detail and coverage of the men's experiences and as such what lies ahead may be triggering for some. It is not my intention to exacerbate distress, so please exercise discretion where needed.

Bradford, UK Russell Delderfield

Acknowledgements

Firstly, to Grace Jackson for believing in my work enough to arrange peer-review and take on the monograph and to Jo O'Neill for taking me through my first foray in solo authorship. Their friendly and approachable professionalism has been very much appreciated. We all have to start somewhere, and it helps if learning the ropes of academic publishing is less a tribulation and more an enjoyable learning curve.

Dr Anne White gave me a job at the university that enabled me to take the first practical steps towards my dream of doing research. She also taught me the essentials of academia back in the day. Thanks for your patience and faith in me. Dr Clare Beckett-Wrighton's support, wisdom and feedback helped me to take the plunge and do the PhD I'd always wanted to study. She has been a steadfast supporter and friend, my thanks go to her too.

Thanks to Sam Thomas who introduced me to charity trustee work and taught me the importance of being part of using our knowledge and skills for change.

Thank you to three wonderful colleagues: the Other Dr Cross, Helen McHattie (Ms. Jackson to her friends), and Lucy Scott. I really could not have gotten through this work without your support. The friendship and forbearance you have shown me has gone way beyond the call of duty of co-workers and I am truly grateful.

My thanks go to Dr Anne, the original academic (her alias being 'Professor Anne Graham'). I talked and talked … and talked about the content of this thesis-turned-book, and she listened and tried to understand its importance and meaning. She also liberally supplied gin and tonic and fizz where it was most needed.

Finally, to Josh, Gareth, James, and Richard. This work would not exist if people were not brave enough to put themselves out there by getting involved in research. My heartfelt thanks go to you for sending me your stories.

Contents

CHAPTER 1

Why Study Men?

Abstract Background to the book is elucidated, both personal and empirical and a rationale is established. Current research findings are considered with emphasis on the few qualitative studies on male eating disorders. Concepts such as stigma, gender role conflict, and muscularity-oriented disordered eating are introduced, the latter being peculiar to the male experience. A summary of the reflexive research design is provided.

Keywords Male eating disorders • Muscle dysmorphia • Qualitative psychology • Interpretative research • Stories • Reflexivity

There are two oft-used openings to research studies on male eating disorders. As papers intone, some of the earliest recorded cases of eating disorders were in men, despite the women-centric trends of the twentieth century. The other is to state that knowledge about males is non-existent or scant at best. These two have become something of a research article cliché.

Cliché or not, to say that anywhere from ten to twenty-five percent of eating disorder cases are male (Sweeting et al. 2015), boys and men are regularly overlooked when it comes to research focus and funding (Murray et al. 2017). Even with our poor handle on prevalence, this still represents many lives affected by these disorders that are known to have high mortality rates (Smink et al. 2012). Therefore, there is a research-informed justification: men are marginalised and we need to know more. However,

R. Delderfield, *Male Eating Disorders*,
https://doi.org/10.1007/978-3-030-02535-9_1

as I am about to argue, it is not enough to know 'more of the same'. For male eating disorders research to advance, diversification of approach is required. I propose qualitative research as being one way to achieve this.

Qualitative research does not seek to assess variables on scales or measures, rather it attempts to understand the meaning of people's experiences without reducing these to statistical values about aetiology, epidemiology, psychopathology or treatment. This type of experiential research is necessary because an over-reliance on a narrow set of methods for knowledge generation has led to glaring gender disparity:

> Socio-cultural constructs of eating disorders have been illuminated by feminist theory, but the lack of equivalent discourse addressing male gender identity has left our knowledge of eating disorders in men aetiolated. (Jones and Morgan 2010: 29)

I take this statement as a call-to-action. As a crude but useful comparison, if I wish to find in-depth critical analyses of women's experiences of anorexia nervosa, their personal stories, and what these reveal about disordered eating and society, I can locate decades of these going back to the 1980s. The same cannot be said about men and it is holding us back. Likewise, I could list male-subject studies that make mention of socio-cultural factors but there are relatively few that actually explore these in any detail (Rodgers et al. 2012; Turel et al. 2018). In short, whilst the study of male eating disorders has, since the first substantial work on the topic (Andersen 1990), stressed the biopsychosocial nature of these conditions, the 'social' bit at the end seems to, well … drop off the end entirely.

The aim of this book is to present my modest attempt to tackle this. I set out to explore the experiences of men, achieving depth through the lens of what we know socially and culturally about men. Of course, this book is not able to generate an entire 'equivalent discourse' (this would be an enormous task) but it is a beginning step in understanding what men live through, in a way that moves beyond psychiatric data, instead adopting a social psychological approach.

A full comprehensive critical review of literature is beyond the scope of the book and, arguably, this has recently been rendered unnecessary by Murray et al. (2017) who have published this to a high standard (I recommend reading). It is important to make something clear. I am not dismissing the literature that emanates from clinical research. Such work is invaluable and is essential to prevention and treatment. It is included here as I introduce evidence that is pertinent in later chapters. However, I will focus on that which truly is scarce within our field: experiential qualitative research.

The Research Story

Now that diagnostic criteria have been redefined to eliminate biological sex-related symptoms, such as the outdated criterion of menstruation cessation from the anorexia classification, it is reported that the presenting issues across the main disorders (anorexia, bulimia, and binge-eating disorder) are essentially the same. This is borne out by studies that focus on psychopathological features. For instance, personal control and its related issues are found to be similar (Cohn and Lemberg 2014; Kelly et al. 2018). Both anorexia and bulimia tend to feature the personality trait perfectionism (Núñez-Navarro et al. 2012). In the development and diagnosis of binge-eating disorder there are few differences to be found (Shingleton et al. 2015). Similarly, men with anorexia develop osteoporosis (Mehler et al. 2018). ‘Pro-Ana’ and ‘pro-Mia’ online spaces, populated by women seeking to sustain their anorexia or bulimia as a lifestyle choice, are now supporting male participants (Turja et al. 2017).

This can be contrasted with findings that, regardless of the improved inclusivity of diagnostic criteria and treatments, emphasise the differences. The following examples illustrate this. A key difference is in prevalence. Men continue to be less likely to develop disordered eating (Sweeting et al. 2015). Disordered eating men are still said to have a less deleterious body image than women (Núñez-Navarro et al. 2012). Despite purported similarity, osteoporosis in male anorexia has a profound difference: the levels of bone mass deterioration was found to be worse, even if they had been starving for shorter durations (Mehler et al. 2018).

Causes, Diagnosis, and Treatment

In terms of what leads to a man experiencing disordered eating, consensus states that causes are largely similar to women (Cohn and Lemberg 2014). Earlier I mentioned the biopsychosocial model. This model covers broad socio-cultural factors, for example cultural expectations or the influence of mass media; local and biological factors, such as familial practices around food and eating, through to our inherited genetics; and individual psychological factors, for example, experience of personal trauma, personality traits or deficits in self-esteem. Certain of these elements are said to have gender distinctions, however.

For example, a history of physical, rather than sexual, abuse in the form of domestic violence indicated future problems with eating (Mitchell et al. 2011). Furthermore, in an investigation about influences on eating behaviours, rather than media images being found to impact, there is some evidence that men's behaviours are more influenced by their friendship groups' comments. This can result in experimenting with the use of strategies that become damaging, such as fasting or eating and purging (Forney et al. 2012). This has not prevented studies from mentioning the media's part in the development of disordered eating, although this remains largely unexplored. A notable exception is a study that focuses specifically on the effects of social media on men's body dissatisfaction and its links with eating disorder symptoms.

Body dissatisfaction is the concept of men being unhappy with their bodies, thin or fat, fit or unfit (Feltman and Ferraro 2011) and it can extend to any aspect of the body, such as height, hair, musculature, chest, legs, buttocks or penis-size. It was asserted that exposure to imagery are related to greater dissatisfaction and adaptive responses in sexual minority men (Griffiths et al. 2018). A final example of difference, is the propensity for male athletes to succumb to disordered eating, depending on expectation within their sport. Wrestlers, swimmers, track running and horse racing, along with instances in football and rugby are said to have increased susceptibility (Blair et al. 2017; Mehler and Andersen 2017).

Men appear to be harder to diagnose (Griffiths et al. 2015). Differential diagnosis is common, with men being assigned to an atypical category. This is often referred to as 'Otherwise Specified Feeding or Eating Disorder' (Smink et al. 2014) in research that is informed by the Diagnostic Statistical Manual (American Psychiatric Association 2013). Male patients may not have a recognisable 'a drive for thinness' (Murray et al. 2017 transition) or be below underweight thresholds. This drive is usually found to some degree, even in non-anorexia disorders. We know, for instance, that clinicians sometimes fail to diagnose eating disorders because, apart from anorexia, men may not appear greatly underweight or overweight (Bayes and Madden 2011), and overweight men are routinely not referred for an eating disorder consultation (MacCaughelty et al. 2016). Problems with diagnosis are compounded by men avoiding health professionals.

Denial, shame and stigma, due to a fear of being perceived as feminine, function as obstacles to accessing help (Cohn and Lemberg 2014; Mehler and Andersen 2017).

Men themselves may fail to perceive that they have problem behaviours (Burlew and Shurts 2013), believing themselves to be idiosyncratic or 'different'. Eating disorders are shameful (Muise et al. 2003) and involve a great deal of secrecy (Delderfield 2013; Ray 2004) but this is 'amplified' in men because "men are reluctant to admit to having a 'women's problem'" (Corson and Andersen 2002: 196). This conceptualisation as a 'female illness' is not limited to a single study. Rather, it appears repeatedly throughout the epidemiological and therapeutic literature (Bartlett and Mitchell 2015; Bryant-Jefferies 2005; Costin 2007; Harvey and Robinson 2003; Raevuori et al. 2008; Räisänen and Hunt 2014; Smart 2006).

Whilst gender-based therapy has been advocated for in the services that men can access (Greenberg and Schoen 2008), the literature is broadly in favour of the view that services are "failing to reflect the gender diversity of the populations which they serve" (Morgan 2013: 277) because they are based on models that were designed around the majority of patients, women (Cohn and Lemberg 2014). Male self-help groups can be useful in proving to men that they are not alone in their condition (Russell and Laszlo 2013). Russell and Laszlo observe about their male-only space: "… offering men a space to talk about emotions can feel a bit like trying to get a cat to swim, technically it can do it, but it is not the done thing for a cat" (2013: 253). The question as to whether all-male treatments are truly effective in tackling perceived barriers by encouraging men to engage in tailored treatment is redundant as there are so few services (in the UK, at least), that it is impossible to tell.

Actual outcomes for men, in terms of symptom abatement, were thought to be better than women in terms of the remission of purging and restoration of weight (Støving et al. 2011). Nevertheless, men are reported to suffer greater overall functional impairment (Striegel et al. 2012), as such the symptoms may have abated but more men leave treatment having reached medical thresholds for 'health' but they continue to experience a poor quality of life, when compared with recovered women (Mitchison et al. 2013). Directly related to this is mortality: the death rate amongst men, after being discharged from treatment for anorexia, remains higher than that of women (Gueguen et al. 2012).

The Threat of Femininity

Returning to an idea that was introduced briefly above, it has been reported in studies about stigma towards eating disorders that having anorexia was thought to be less masculine (Griffiths et al. 2013). Similar findings occur for bulimia. This extends further: men with any eating disorder are assumed, by others, to be non-heterosexual (Essayli et al. 2018). Men display more stigma than women about the illness; they believe that the sufferer is personally responsible for their bulimia (McLean et al. 2014). This experience switches our focus from a purely psychiatric psychologising of male eating disorders to something that is more societally ingrained (Ray 2004). A fear of being 'feminised' suggests something far more pervasive than an unhealthy relationship with food and body. It appears to suggest that eating disorders challenge the very essence of identity, of a man's masculinity (including sexuality) itself, which is something that remains under-analysed in the literature I have drawn on so far.

In his analysis of the causes of male eating disorders, Andersen suggests that "…young men are confronted daily with a definition of manhood which is distorted, dysfunctional, and potentially destructive" (1990: 63). The psychological theory that has been tested in the literature which explains the effects with such a toxic version of what it means to be a 'man' is Gender Role Conflict (GRC). This theory propounds that one's gender role is ascribed and is built upon perceived expectations of two constructs, femininity and masculinity. It certainly seems that there is a link between issues around feeling and being 'masculine' and efforts to control and change body image (O'Dea and Abraham 2002). GRC extends beyond biological indicators to the psychological messages we receive and retain about gender. Gender-related reinforcement appears to have greater effect on our eating and body-related behaviours than biological sex (Andersen and DiDomenico 1992). Good and Wood (1995) found there to be a strong link between GRC and attitudes about seeking help and support. Men who felt as if they had failed to be 'proper men' saw themselves in a poor light and were less likely to get help when needed.

Failure to be a 'man' included feeling a tension between living up to a 'macho' persona and "sensitive, introspective leanings" (Andersen 1985: 156). Potential inculcated hyper-masculine roles have been analysed in relation to the function of men's bodies on television. McCabe and Ricciardelli (2004) proposed three depictions for modern man: tool, weapon or object of gaze. This suggests that men, like women, are exposed to a narrow scope of what their bodies mean to them and others. Our bodies are no longer biological matter, instead "…the male body … is a punishing crucible in which the ego is painfully subjected to the tyranny of the ideal" (Gilmore 1994: 214). However, an earlier analysis offered a broader manifestation than a purely bodily expression of being a man, instead suggesting that men had to conform to five archetypes: as soldier, lord, frontiersman, expert, breadwinner (Hesse-Biber 1996). These have become increasingly difficult to live up to as not one of these is the preserve of men alone anymore; there is a suggestion that men are experiencing "emasculation" (Robinson et al. 2013: 176).

Eating disorder psychiatrists have suggested that 'maleness' and 'femaleness' are very different from one another within Western society (Andersen 1995) but the discussions in these analyses are biological, about sex, not about the 'gender' of gender role conflict implied in this experience of emasculation. This theory of a conflict in men's gender role clearly reaches way beyond the psychiatric process involved in acquiring, diagnosing and treating an eating disorder. However, in the eating disorders literature it still takes the form of a syndrome or detectable individualised struggle that is pathologised in the search for causes of male eating disorder (Botha 2012).

Perhaps, however, Andersen's idea has credence: it is the biological difference of a male body that appears to be at the heart of recent body-change behaviours. As men's gender difference from women has diminished in the face of equality this has left men casting about for an identity that is discernibly masculine. This is a topic that the eating disorders and body image literature attempts to engage with. A visible, openly displayed form of masculinity which is utterly unlike 'being a woman' is that very biological difference: the male body (Baghurst et al. 2006; Olivardia 2002). This in turn is internalised as a prevailing notion of successful masculinity that repudiates femininity (Maine and Bunnell 2008) and failure to attain this may result in "An irrational conviction of a defective masculine body" which may ultimately manifest as an eating disorder (Halperin 1996: 161).

Muscularity-Oriented Disordered Eating (MODE)

Bodybuilding is no longer the preserve of a semi-professional group of men. Recreational bodybuilding through gym-going, means that more men are investing time in changing and re-shaping their bodies (Devrim et al. 2018; Mitchell et al. 2017). A study investigating a community sample resulted in a rudimentary hypothetical model of the relationship between a drive for thinness, muscularity, body-change behaviours and negative affect in young men (Rodgers et al. 2012). Whilst this model does seem to reduce a complex web of socio-cultural constructs to little more than a diagram of measurable 'co-efficients', there is an observation that a damaging psychological condition can arise when a drive for a muscular body goes awry by becoming obsessive. When the desire for a hyper-masculine, muscular body becomes psychologically damaging because for the man no amount of muscle is enough, this has emerged as muscle dysmorphia.

Muscle dysmorphia may appear to be a detour in a discussion about male eating disorders but this consuming pursuit of muscularity is pertinent in two ways. Firstly, it has recently been posited that, rather than being a dysmorphia, as a disorder its relationship with food, the body and psychological problems means that it has more in common with eating disorders (Compte et al. 2018). MODE is currently the subject of significant debate but one of its distinguishing features is that it is more prevalent in men than women (Murray et al. 2016). Secondly, it highlights the role of the male body in the development of disordered behaviour. A debilitating obsession with muscularity among men is not new. Morgan (2000) finds mention of a similar condition with the same symptoms as far back as 1969. However, for our purposes the concept originated in studies that began the exploration of bodybuilders' body image. Pope et al. (1993) studied a sample of 108 bodybuilders and made a comparison between traditional anorexia and something they referred to as 'reverse anorexia nervosa'. The similarities between anorexia and muscle dysmorphia are difficult to ignore. Both women with anorexia and men with reverse anorexia had similar psychological traits, including but not limited to obsessive compulsions, perfectionism, anhedonia, narcissism (Davis and Scott-Robertson 2000) and ideal body/self-internalisation (Grieve 2007), though the former group was labelled as 'disordered' at the time, while the latter was not.

Although Pope and colleagues framed muscle dysmorphia as being a specific sub-category of body dysmorphic disorder (a condition in which the sufferer's obsessive self-perception of their own looks is pathologically distorted), their research subjects did not (Pope et al. 2005; Pope Jr. et al. 1997). One participant, Kevin, called the condition he experienced 'bigorexia' (Pope et al. 2000: 84) a term that seems to have been in use in the gym community (Mosley 2009). Bigorexia results in sustained and damaging relationships with food, diet and supplements, and all associated behaviours. This includes restrictive and excessive behaviours, all under the guise of optimum nutrition for muscle-gain. Men may follow rigid and uncompromising diets. Indeed, some of the disruption to social and family life is often due not only to training regimes but to having to prepare and consume highly specific meal plans (Lantz et al. 2002).

At other times men may deliberately eat to excess. This is sometimes called 'bulking and cutting' and involves dosing on supplements, protein and moderate carbohydrates in large quantities to be stored by the body for later transformation into muscle mass (Brill and Keane 1994; Karimian and Esfahani 2011; Peixoto Labre 2002). This can set up a cycle of vulnerable self-esteem and distorted self-perception as they gain excess weight during bulking prior to 'cutting' (a process whereby muscles are increased and diet lowers subcutaneous lipids to achieve maximum definition), where previous mass and tone appear to be lost. This is not to suggest, however, that all people who practise bodybuilding through weight-lifting will automatically be muscle dysmorphic. There is a final observation to offer that supports Murray et al.'s (2016) assertion about the increasing societal value of muscle. The appeal and elevated status of the hyper-mesomorphic male body is so pervasive that young children, both boys and girls, now demonstrate a preference for muscle-laden dolls, referred to as 'action figures' (as goodness forbid we should suggest that boys be not action-oriented). Children prefer hyper-muscular versions of these toys because, and I am paraphrasing here, 'muscles are better' (Baghurst et al. 2018).

Almost all of the research that has been explored so far uses statistical analyses to present data and interpret findings. In some cases, data collection has been through an inherently more personal method, such as interviewing. In others, previous records have been retrospectively examined and mined for insights and patterns. That said, most studies employed instruments that were designed to get people to respond using questionnaires, surveys and scales. This is a misleading use of language on my part because I actually mean eating disordered women, rather than people. In fact, when these same surveys and questionnaires have been used on males the results have proven far less reliable. Lock likens this to "trying to fit square pegs in round holes" (2009: 99). All the right pieces may be there but they are just not fitting together. It has been posited that these questionnaires may be worded in ways that reflect a female experience, for example by having a focus on female body shape such as hips and thighs

(Boerner et al. 2004) and that introduce bias or skew the findings (Gila et al. 2005). Lower reliability on instruments like these is being flagged "constantly" (Dakanalis and Riva 2013: 198) and there have been calls for the development of validated, reliable instruments to detect and measure pathology for use with men (Murray et al. 2010) because "continuing to view EDs through the lens of female gender means we risk omitting important information about the male experience..." (Darcy 2011: 311).

Researchers and clinicians have duly responded. Newer measures that are designed for both sexes are being tested, such as the Eating Pathology Symptoms Inventory (EPSI, Forbush et al. 2014). An instrument specifically for males has recently been piloted and published. The Eating Disorder Assessment for Men (EDAM), a 50-item Likert scale self-report questionnaire, is a new and promising addition to the suite of clinical and research tools (Cohn and Lemberg 2014) and further validation will determine its future value. These male-specific developments have been over a decade in the making. The need to subject instruments to scrutiny had been previously proposed, to assess "...whether they can accurately capture men's experiences" (Tylka and Subich 2002: 277). However, I would add '...or whether they can capture experience at all'. This may seem overtly critical but the fact remains: give someone a questionnaire and they may answer but we will not really know anything beyond what was asked on the questionnaire.

Qualitative Beginnings

Qualitative research deliberately sets out to capture the experiences of men without intention to measure frequency, identify and manipulate variables or assess statistical power. There are so few of these studies pertaining to men that I can briefly incorporate findings from them all.

An individual in-depth exploration using heuristic self-analysis was one of the qualitative studies that inspired my own story. It charts a man's descent into eating disorder and the conditions required for subsequent recovery. Campling (2012) uses a creative self-exploration, rather than a conveyor belt of psychiatric studies, to understand the personal and socio-cultural factors that he exposed as he questioned and used scholarly literature to make sense of his life with anorexia. This illuminates critical points in his experience, such as the importance and personal significance of puberty in the onset of his disorder, along with the notion of an eating disorder as a mechanism that 'colonises' the individual until very little of his self is left. His findings conceptualise recovery as either ‘complete’ or ‘compromised’ but not ‘cured’.

Some socio-cultural factors have been studied qualitatively. Media and social influences were identified as causing part of body dissatisfaction among men, finding few differences between gay and straight men in this regard (Morgan and Arcelus 2009). However, the locus of the disorder was still framed as being within the male and the key issues around interpreting the form and nature of what these media are and how they influence was not in scope. These findings were somewhat contradicted by a study that conducted biographical interviews boys with eating disorder diagnoses and their families. Analysis of these interviews challenged the media-centric and media-propagated notion that body image was directly responsible for a rise in disordered eating in males. It was found that boys did not appear to aspire to be hyper-masculine bodies to the point of dysfunction, in their eating disorder stories, other elements took priority. The heterogeneity of the boys’ experiences was emphasised, rather than a homogenous media myth about males becoming ill because they strove for the perfect body (Wright et al. 2016).

The uniqueness of each man’s experience was also the summative finding of an earlier study that tried to represent men’s voices, reporting that “…a complex tapestry of emotions, issues, trends, and themes emerged from the stories of the men interviewed.” Ahonen (2003: 15). Far more convincingly than other clinical studies, this paper was able to demonstrate the substantial connection between food intake or restriction and emotional states in the men that were reported on. Using the themes of shame, isolation and low self-esteem but recording the very different experiences reported by the interviewees, this work concludes that if psychiatry is seeking a blueprint of a man-with-eating-disorder, then this is a mistaken venture.

There have been qualitative attempts to bringing experiential findings to a clinical audience. A published life story about John Evans (2011) anorexia was analysed and digested for health professionals. John’s experiences of his vanished libido’s return, as an indicator of recovery, was discussed. So too was his shame and the stigma he encountered. An under-explored element in the clinical literature, men’s use of over-exercising as a compensatory, compulsive response, was highlighted. John’s story represented something missing in the body of research to which nurses are routinely exposed: the voice of the men these disorders affect. This was presented as important because it provides something that cannot be gleaned from detached scientific studies; the actual pain, suffering and mental processes that a man goes through when he is 'trapped' on an all-female ward being treated for something he refused to believe he had Dalgliesh and Nutt (2013).

Recently this has been added to with an interview study with clinicians about their views on adapting treatments for men. Whilst the clinicians acknowledged that men presented with some gender-specific features despite the broad similarities around diagnosis and symptoms between men and women, they said they would not necessarily change treatments to work with these features. One participant is reported as saying that they would use standard models that are usually "tailored to the individual rather than the gender or the sexuality or the race." (Kinnaird et al. 2018: 3). This oxymoron captures one of the fundamental issues at the heart of some clinical practitioners' understandings of identity. How can something be tailored to an individual without incorporating aspects that may be fundamental to their experience of being one? Race, sexual orientation or living in one's own skin as man or woman are surely an integral experience of self. I would be keen to know how these models are tailored for individuals if they deliberately set aside key aspects of an individual's existence.

As opposed to work with clinicians, men's perspectives as patients were gathered through interviews, too. These included feeling aware that men with eating disorders were "invisible" (Robinson et al. 2013: 5) and that they feared a negative response upon telling others about their disorder. This included not wanting employers to know because of a risk of being judged unable to cope and ruining career chances. There was also a difficult paradox that men had to grapple with. Namely, accepting the disorder as a damaging problem, while it was still being experienced as the solution. This involved identity work, the disorder had made them feel 'acceptable' and the more that his was challenged, the more the men were left with feelings of just how 'unacceptable' they were at a fundamental level.

Interviewing also revealed that successful recovery is enhanced by immediate relief from destructive behaviours, with a longer-term plan that addresses issues around social re-integration and personal restoration. Men experienced the need for change, which involved admitting that they had a problem, along with committing to letting go of the eating disorder and finding new ways to relate to other people in their lives (Pettersen et al. 2016). Full recovery was experienced but it involved significant work on personal self-worth and body acceptance in a way to which men had not previously been accustomed. Learning how to incorporate exercise without compulsion and how to deprioritise others' perceptions and opinions, in favour of being more self-prioritising and autonomous also emerged as important experiences (Björk et al. 2012).

Thematic analysis of facilitating an all-male self-help group likened men to "lone-wolves" (Russell and Laszlo 2013: 252) and found that men struggled with their masculinity, feeling pressure to be a 'man' but not in ways that were aggressive, unfriendly or demeaning to others. Yet, there were still feelings attached to being perceived as feminised. Taking the step to get treatment engendered fear of being seen as 'feeble' or female and initial contact with health practitioners did little to assuage this. One man was told that he should 'man-up' and stop being weak by his doctor. This was coupled with being given medical information that still felt devoid of symptoms and advice that would apply to men, such as being leaflets about side effects that covered anorexia's impact on the female body and reproduction (Räisänen and Hunt 2014).

The feminised nature of male anorexia, mentioned above, has been studied using discourse analysis to analyse the disorder from a sociological perspective (Till 2011). It is argued that the discourses around anorexia as fundamentally feminised and that these are pathologised as being 'bad' and 'ill'. As a result, men are handed a feminine identity when they are identified as having anorexia and in need of help. Till investigates the occurrence of societally-pervasive psychiatric discourses that make anorexia synonymous of femininity and femininity synonymous of weakness, to the point that men fear that they have a 'woman's illness'. This insight relates to something more unsettling that I have pointed out in other work:

> Why is having a "women's illness" such a bad thing? Let's suppose an eating disorder really was a "women's issue" then, eating disorder aside, what have we done to our men to make them believe that being anything like a woman is bad or something to feel ashamed about? Apparently, we are in complete denial about the sexism that continues to be deeply instilled in boys by the society that's supposed to nurture and enlighten them. (Delderfield 2014)

Unfortunately, what lies ahead in this book is unable to answer these questions, and this 'feminine-as-flawed' continues to be a cause for concern.

The Personal Story

My first 'symptoms' (as they would later be called) appeared in the school year 1989–1990, however, I was not diagnosed with bulimia nervosa until April 2003, almost fourteen years later. My doctor was pro-active in getting a referral to a specialised psychotherapist, given the state of chaos I was in at the time, with my ability to function increasingly spiralling out of my control. It did not feel as if this was enough; I wanted to understand more than the one-page print-out of generic information my GP had given me at the end of our first consultation. I began to cast about for more guidance on what this diagnosis meant and what I should do to get better.

I felt alone and isolated and I wondered if there were groups to support people in my situation. The Eating Disorders Association (now *Beat*) had a helpline so I telephoned to ask for information, only to be told that they did not offer any specific resources aimed at men. They did send me some information about support groups but the nearest one was 'female-only'. This is how my burgeoning realisation began that men with an eating disorder were so exceptional at the time that they had been "legislated out of existence" (Andersen 1995: 177). I desperately wanted to know if other men had experienced anything like what I was going through.

At the time, the Internet yielded very little. There were some online chat rooms and discussion boards. What I did find were books. Some men had written their life stories down and had them published (Brooks 1997; Bruni 2009; Campling 2007; Cuban 2013; Evans 2011; Grahl 2007; Holbrook 2000; Kohl 2009; Krasnow 1996; Leith 2010; McBride 2014; Murphy-Robinson 2007; Nolan 2008; Prager 2010; Ruiz 2008; Samuel 2008; Saxen 2007; Simon 2006; Wilps 1990). These affirmed that I was not alone, that writing a life story could convey incredible insights into the eating disorder and inspired me to attempt something similar. What follows was written in a single sitting in 2008 but it has been recently edited for length.

> My destructive relationship with food had taken a noticeable grip by the time I was fourteen. My family focused heavily on a perfectionist driver, including wanting to keep us as children, like Peter Pan. When I and my sibling entered puberty this was hard on my parents as they wanted us to not grow up and begin changing. I finally sought professional help when I realised that all my attempts to 'cure' myself were making me more and more ill—not better.

In my early life I had experienced embargoes on certain foods, not because they were bad for us but because they belonged to my parents and we were not allowed to have them. In a typically northern way, 'healthy' food comprised of meat and vegetable dinners with the vegetables cooked until they were little more than mush. Whilst we were not given fast-food a great deal, comforting carbohydrates were often a principle food source. Suet puddings, bread served with any/every meal and Friday treats of large cakes frequently featured.

My family script consisted of being perfect, pleasing people, not displaying difficult emotions and taking care of others. This was juxtaposed against my mother's assertion that it was OK to talk about anything at all with my parents; in reality, when I attempted this, they struggled to talk about difficult subjects. They would accuse me of being far too emotional or put my fears, concerns and tears down to my hormones. My hormones were used to explain a plethora of things between the ages of twelve and twenty.

I had noticed my unpleasant body-shape in a pre-pubescent photo of my brother and I sitting, shirtless whilst on a picnic, with my great aunt, on a hot summer's day. That picture is still the first time I knew I didn't look 'right'. From a very young age, around seven or eight, I hated having my photo taken and refused to smile as I thought I looked awful when I fully smiled, instead I adopted a thin, tight-lipped grin whenever I did have to be in a photo.

It was also around this age when I first began experiencing crushes on other boys. At secondary school it felt overwhelming as everything hit at once. I discovered many things all at the same time. The first being that I wasn't like other children. I apparently (according to what I have been told) had an old head on young shoulders ('mature beyond his years' frequently appeared on school reports). People wanted to talk to me about their troubles. I became adept at keeping secrets. I was also given labels such as 'individual' or 'quirky'. Despite these perceptions of me, I was lucky enough to avoid serious bullying, in fact I had one of my early sexual experiences with one of the 'hardest' boys at school who then became my 'protector' and shielded me from much of this. However, I was still terrified of 'individual and quirky' being replaced by being called gay.

In retrospect, I lived in a permanent state of fear and spent much of my puberty in a state of emotional hijack. Some of my principle fears revolved around the paper-round which I was forced to take on by my parents due to their strong work ethic. This became a weekly dose of terror. I used to take a pound of my previous week's money, begin my round at the shop where I would buy chocolate bars and eat them all on my way around the scary area I delivered to, frightened of the gangs of other children hanging about and the strangers' houses that had dogs in them. My greatest fear, however, was not that weekly torture but concealing my diaries, detailing my crushes on other boys.

I was mortified when my body became masculine, practically overnight, I did not feel as masculine as I was beginning to look. I was aware that I did not have a desire to be feminine, just not so utterly manly. I had hair everywhere and was being teased by the time I was twelve for having a moustache and beard, so I made the decision to shave it off. To make this experience worse my father found out and was furious, shouting at me and storming around the house, telling me that it was ridiculous that I should be shaving at my age and demanding to know what I was trying to prove. It was awful because he made it sound as if I wanted to do it, to prove how grown up I was, when in reality it was the opposite. I began getting up earlier than Dad every morning so that I was ready for school before he even got out of bed to get ready for work. It was confusing and tiring and I hoarded treats bought with my paper round money to help me through. The abundance of secret eating led to weight gain, which ramped up my turmoil further: boys would never fancy me if I was flabby. I was avoiding sport like the plague whilst being fed like an adult man because I was, apparently, 'built like my dad' (which I was told so many times it still plays on a loop in my mind sometimes). I dreaded Physical Education (as many teenagers do) because we were made to play skins-on-shirts often. Just the fact that everyone would see how fat and hairy I was, was frightening enough.

The 'relationships' I had with boys were desperately wanted but seemed to lead to bouts of further confusion and pain. My experiences with them filled my mind permanently. It was as if there were no escape. The only time I felt numb was when I ate. What was so difficult was that I did 'attract' boys. Some of them initiated physical contact but this seemed to be followed by a period of guilt and coldness on their behalf, making me feel rejected and as if I had imagined their attraction. A particular 'relationship' like this was agony for years. After we originally had physical contact over the course of a school year, exchanged little 'love' notes, gone for long bicycle rides together to 'get away from everyone else', this boy, crimson-faced, told me one afternoon that he loved me and asked if I loved him. When I told him that I did, I remember feeling utterly thrilled. Ultimately, when I next saw him in school he merely said 'hello' and from then on blanked and did not want to see me when I called around to his house for him until I had 'gotten the message'.

In spite of these encounters, I had a degree of 'popularity' at school, was able to get on with my teachers and with my peers and navigate my way through it. I increasingly projected a 'non-sexuality' and only allowed 'safe' inner expressions of my sexuality. I did not show interest in girls, nor did I show overt interest in boys, no matter what people suspected. By the time I left for university I had honed my skills for listening to other people and suppressed any display of my inner feelings. Having always had an effeminacy and sense of humour, I developed a persona as a 'non-threatening gay man' when I did come out at uni. People found it easy to develop friendships with me and I was convinced that this was due to my being honest about my sexuality but wholly reliant on my not expressing it.

University brought about two main changes in the development of my eating disorder and my sexuality simultaneously. I was let loose on my own life, meaning I was able to eat exactly what I wanted when I wanted, no more embargoes or home-made stews! All those things I had been denied at home I could have them … in abundance. I lost complete control with this. I also met another guy who lived in my halls of residence and fell in love. He told me, on several occasions, that he loved me, too. Unfortunately, inexperienced as my heart was, it broke quickly and thoroughly when he made it clear that he did not want to pursue a relationship with me. For the first time in my entire life I experienced what it was like to not have an appetite. I forgot to eat, so engulfed was I by pain. My weight came off rapidly and suddenly I discovered that I could look different, that I could have a different body shape. As I recovered from my heartache my appetite gradually returned and, in fact, felt as if it increased. I resumed protective eating but had discovered a new dimension to food—not eating. I would give up eating properly for days to counteract the effects of a binge and so my weight varied drastically for the next few years.

Being out about my sexuality also came with a sting in its tail. I quickly arrived at a destructive realisation. In the past, I could console myself that I had not found a loving relationship because my experiences were clandestine in nature; things happened but were not acknowledged or talked about. Now I was open about myself and was beginning to meet other men who were also 'out'. However, I was repeatedly told that I was fat and that no-one would fancy me. This cemented my long-standing deeply-internalised dialogues that I was unattractive and was not meant to be a sexual being who deserved love. I simply was not fanciable, men wanted to know me but this was because I was funny and a good friend.

I entered a period of 'insanity', my moods became increasingly erratic showing compassion, kindness, empathy and good-humour punctuated with explosive rages directed at someone over a minor issue. At the same time, I began to use laxatives to purge my body of the absolute junk I forced into it during a binge. This insanity gathered pace when I began to exercise, at first it felt unnatural then I noticed the effect on my body-shape and began to feel anxious if I couldn't get to a class. So I doubled up, then I trebled up—taking three classes back to back each day.

There was a noticeable nadir. I felt it when I was in it, it felt like madness and I was out of control. I took a nutrition course, qualified in fitness and began teaching exercise classes. Now I taught hours of classes and joined several gyms so that I could do workouts without anyone asking why I was there so much. I would calculate calories so I could make accurate calculations of binges and do sufficient exercise to burn this off, whilst taking laxatives to make sure that I was getting rid of the bloated feeling as soon as possible, so that I could still study and work. My desire for a relationship and my sex drive were eclipsed by food and exercise. I thought of nothing else.

I noticed a change in how men perceived me and found that they were attracted to me but now I feared any sort of intimacy, let alone sex, as I was terrified they'd discover how disgusting and mad I was. I was even scared that if I found a significant relationship now it would ruin me because I would not have privacy to binge nor the time to exercise as much as I needed to counteract it. Instead, having been sure for years that what I wanted was a close, lasting, mutual relationship with another man, I began having meaningless promiscuous encounters which felt hollow and were, at times, dangerous because of the risks I took. I was convinced I should be thankful to have anyone showing me any sort of attention, given how odd I was.

My therapist, years later, helped me to realise that the end result of these weekend sexual binges were food binges during my working week. As I managed to give up purging (which is one of the hardest things I have ever done), I became increasingly withdrawn. The more weight I gained, the more I could only bear to leave the house for work. Many friendships deteriorated during this time, as I deliberately stayed home alone licking my wounds—now that I had a clearer idea of what wounds I bore. I even had time off work on the days when I particularly could not bear the thought of anyone having to look at me, I knew they would find me offensive to look at.

My partial recovery was marked by this phase of giving up purging and tackling bingeing. Although I felt an enormous relief, having validation that I wasn't abnormal or mad, as my obsession with food (consuming it or starving myself) was challenged this gave way to an abyss of self-loathing. Whilst I had the skills to manage my relationships with other people or to help them manage themselves, I did not have the skills to deal with the depth of hatred and disgust I felt towards myself. My social isolation has gradually ended since. As I worked to understand how my bulimic-to-binger-self fit with the rest of me, I wanted to know more about others' experiences. For instance, I sought to understand how a human being from a loving family (I should say at this point that I do believe that—that my parents always meant well and were simply trying to do their best) can become ingrained with such destructive coping mechanisms.

Therapeutically, I continue to work for recovery from my bingeing habits and compulsions, this goes hand-in-hand with re-evaluating my self-worth. I am so thoroughly convinced that I am not to be cherished or loved. I have experienced so much rejection that it is my default setting: to assume that accepting me for who I am is simply not a possibility. I have always seen the beauty in others whilst failing to find any beauty whatsoever within me.

As the story shows, I have had a destructive, dangerous and consumingly negative relationship with food (or working to assure the absence of it) throughout most of my life. Although the experience of it has ebbed and flowed with other life experiences it has been my constant companion. As such, my motivation to undertake research in this area arises out of a deeply personal and painful relationship with my own eating disorder that I am actively working to recover from. Whatever research I was able to undertake could not be in the guise of a detached and impersonal analyst, therefore, in addition to being qualitative, my study needed to acknowledge and harness this personal element, not dishonestly deny it.

The Study's Story

The aim of the work appearing in this book was to add qualitative insights to a discipline dominated by quantitatively-derived data in a way that was as unfettered as possible. The study was designed to be exploratory, accessing men's experiences of disordered eating and relating these to the social and cultural context in which they occur. An additional peripheral aim was to understand myself better by situating my own experiences within a broader context of men's lived experience of eating and food distress.

To achieve the aims of the project without producing 'more-of-the-same', I searched for a different approach that could provide the level of freedom required in emergent exploratory research, rather than having to adhere to a prescriptive off-the-shelf methodology (Denscombe 2010; Marshall and Rossman 2011). I am inclined to the assertion by Newton et al. (2012) that the qualitative research community needs to progress beyond continuously justifying the foundation of its methods, something that quantitative researchers feel little compulsion to do. Nevertheless, I will provide brief details about my research design as it adds to the transparency of what follows.

Finding Stories

Determining how to gain access to something which is, at best, a personal topic that might be perceived as socially sensitive (Ellis et al. 1997) or, at worst, something so emotionally painful that coming forward to share that experience is unlikely to occur was a crucial part of my process that had direct impact on my decisions. Although many options for collecting data abound, it seemed overwhelmingly that transcripts generated from interviews were popular and already thoroughly critiqued as a reliable technique for use in qualitative research (Denscombe 2010; Elliott 2005; Wilkinson 2002). Interviewing certainly appeared to be the preferred method used by other qualitative male disordered eating studies to date. However, my personal experience of reading men's published accounts, as well as the persistent mention of 'stories' from interview-method literature (Elliott 2005; Mauthner and Doucet 1998; Silverman 2006; Smith 2008), combined to make me think that perhaps men could literally write their stories. Elliott (2005) suggests that this is made even more desirable as it may afford the chance to record a story, on a man's own terms and in his own time and way. As the very essence of qualitative research is about being attuned to collecting, listening to and telling stories (McLeod 2001) and the idea of a 'storying' runs throughout this chapter in the choice of section titles.

Once I began looking for information on stories-as-data I discovered differing perspectives about what they were able to represent. Rather than perceiving stories as 'true' or 'untrue', Levering expresses this problem as the following question: "how authoritative are people's accounts of their own perceptions?" (2006: 451). This question is particularly cogent when thinking about stories of ourselves. Just the term 'story' in itself is normally evocative of a work of fiction, something creative told to entertain or teach. If this is the case, then Levering's question is meaningful here if a study intends to make a claim to truth using people's stories: how far can they be trusted? To what degree are they real? This is the subject of some debate. Parker cautions against what he terms the "mistaken view" (2005: 75) that there is a story dormant within us, waiting to be discovered by a researcher unearthing the truth. This idea conjures up the image of a researcher simply finding that which is already there: something pre-existing which, although buried, is already constituted, true and complete. So, stories may not be able to offer a guaranteed, easily-validated insight into somebody's world. Nor, of course, do they appear to have a set of controllable 'variables' or easy methods to triangulate their content (Shaughnessy and Zechmeister 2006).

This is assuming, of course, that stories are being gathered in the name of a retrievable, general 'truth' rather than the capturing of a perception of subjective experience. In exploration and interpretative approaches, it is this very subjective experience that we are interested in obtaining. Advances in technology and social-networking have led to the opportunity for life and experience to be written about, and displayed for, friends, family or even the public to read. Some people regularly maintain websites and blogs which capture details of their life events, interests, exploits or hardships. In the case of both oral and written stories, what the story-teller holds is the opportunity to pre-empt the audience receiving the tale; he may edit dependent upon occasion, personal circumstances and hindsight (Fay 1996). He may also use his story to construct a version of himself and his experiences which may perpetuate and bolster a particular self-perception. Alternatively, the storying may be transformative (Wortham 2000), allowing him to renew, refresh or re-present himself (LeVasseur 2003).

I would argue that each story, each version, that makes it into the wider social world through expression is the 'authoritative' version of someone's self-perceptions captured at that specific point and context, constructed for its personal or social meaning and value (Parker 2005). It is authoritative in that it is his own; he has determined the expression as far as was possible. The account can linger as it is or be re-told another day to incrementally or vastly change, adding to or detracting from a person's idea of himself (Fay 1996):

> We invent our stories with a passion, they are momentarily true, we may cling to them, they may become our lives, and then we may move on. Clinging to the story, changing the story, reworking it, denying it. Kenneth Plummer (Mauthner and Doucet 1998: 21)

In other words, stories are constructed to explain and present ourselves; stories we tell ourselves and others contribute to the construction of our self-perception. In this respect, they constitute an individual's current 'truth'. Given this socially constructed worldview, I required a method of analysis that could make sense of our individual and collective meaning-making of life experiences (Burr 2015), something that would also recognise the importance of text in representing snapshots of perceptions of the reality for eating-disordered men.

Contributing Stories

The contributor group was determined by the aims and the research context. UK adult males aged 18 years and over were recruited using a non-probability (Bernard 2012) style of recruitment seemed useful given the design of the study; a large number of men was not needed, which is something relatively common within qualitative research (Silverman 2005). I did not seek contributors who fitted any specific personal requirements, such as age, marital status, sexuality, occupation, class or race. All contributors were briefed on the project, provided a consent statement and given a pseudonym. These are the names that appear in this book.

Other than this, I deliberately avoided collecting demographic information to maximise anonymity and to promote the idea that it was their stories that were being examined, not they themselves. And this is where some researchers begin to feel uncomfortable, I only collected stories. I do not know ages, occupations, relationship and/or disability statuses, race, class or sexual orientation. This may seem an unusual practice to some, as we cling to ideas that arbitrary demographic information will somehow make the data more 'real'. However, the interpretative approach used is one that focuses upon texts and what can be learnt from them once they are separated from their originators. Also, I am working with idiographic experiences; I am not trying to create generalisable nomothetical messages about a larger UK male disordered-eating population, so representativeness was not required. This is also why, when someone refers to the men's stories as 'case studies', I respond that this is erroneous, as case studies tend to come with appropriate situating data. Therefore, requesting demographic data was simply not necessary, I worked with pure text and nothing else. If I information appears about age or sexual orientation, for example, it is because this was volunteered in the text.

The contributors were 'recruited' via a research website that I designed specifically for the purpose hosted by the University of Bradford in the UK. Project details were circulated to two eating disorder charities: *Men Get Eating Disorders Too* and *Beat* once ethical approval for the project was received by my institution. It was made clear that I was interested in hearing from men who self-identified as having experience of disordered eating or with a psychiatric diagnosis of an eating disorder, either were acceptable. Men were required to have basic information technology proficiency and a personal email account, as they were asked to type up their story using word-processing software and attach this to an email to send to me. This process could be completed at a time convenient to them, in an environment that permitted access to a personal computer or other device.

The study aimed to recruit a minimum of four to five contributors. I offered some basic guidance about what an account might include without listing items that would denote specific content and structure. Nor was an example story provided, as this could have set a perceived 'standard'. The men were encouraged to include anything which they felt to be important, things that mattered to them, rather than feeling as if they had to anticipate what I would want to know. I made it clear I was not out to 'prove a particular theory' about men with disordered eating. I emphasised that the story could be in their own words and that I was not going to make any judgements about writing 'ability', grammar or spelling, for instance. I also suggested that the story could be as long as they preferred, explaining that there was no limit on how few or how many words or pages of text could be sent.

Analysing Stories

I decided that an open interpretative approach was best. The analysis was founded upon the premise that "ways of reading are transfigured as ways of researching" (Crotty 1998: 110). Each story was subjected to multiple readings and re-readings, producing four interpretations. These interpretations were inspired by a quadripartite process (Alvesson and Sköldberg 2017). This provided a loose structure for the analytical work, whilst still allowing the freedom to be iterative, moving back and forth between the texts and the interpretations that I was generating. The stories were analysed individually, then in comparison with one another (see Interpretations 1–3, below). No attempt was made to code for themes. Instead, in practical terms, I captured these different interpretations of the stories using interlining (writing directly between the lines of the story). These interlinings were then transposed to produce another copy allowing me to see my interpretations set alongside the original story or entirely detached from the original in a new, individual document. Often these interpretations were left fallow then revisited as more understanding was accrued from the larger body of original texts. 'Reading-in' began to create a fusion of insights from men's published stories and relevant eating disorders literature. This produced Interpretation 4.

- *Interpretation 1—Emotive-Responsive*: I anticipated having a personal, possibly visceral, reaction to reading the stories. I aimed to capture as faithfully as possible my subjective responses, resonances and any automatic thoughts that were evoked alongside the man's text. These were bound to influence my interpretative work and "…a profound level of self-awareness is required to begin to capture the perspectives through which we view the world; and the[se] unconscious filters … cannot be easily grasped" (Mauthner and Doucet

1998: 123). This interpretation helped me to later reflect on whether my line of inquiry around a story was informed by the story itself or my emotional response to it. It supported the integration of researcher-self and reflection as being necessary to the work, without it dominating the overall interpretative endeavour. It also acknowledged that I would have an immediate personal response to each story, rather than operating (disingenuously) as if my first reading would be dispassionate and objective.

- *Interpretation 2—Empathic*: I re-read the story with "openness and receptivity" (Crotty 1998: 109), which involved actively attending to the story being told and trying to tune into the writer's expression of what they may have been going through. This is referred to as 'listening' to the text (Gadamer and Linge 1976). This perspective allowed me to 'distance' myself from my earlier, highly-personalised interpretation but in a way that focused my thinking on identifying their core messages and experiences. In debating the nature of empathy in interpretative understanding, when working with text rather than face-to-face methods, Bénéï (2011) frames empathy as 'being close to' in order to gain an empathic appreciation (McLeod 2010). This is a key aspect of interpretative work: "…to accompany its author as far as you possibly can…" (Bénéï 2011: 877), working with the text to understand the experiences, as they are presented, as fully as possible.
- *Interpretation 3—Probing and Questioning*: this involved "knocking at the text" (Alvesson and Sköldberg 2009: 86), where the stories of disordered eating were questioned. These questions were filtered to include only those that arose from the text, rather than being the product of my unfettered curiosity. Immediate answers to these questions were sought in the experiences documented on the page and in the other stories that had been located (Schleiermacher and Bowie 1998). There is interplay between the story's whole and parts, and the whole and parts of other stories, as answers are sought by moving back and forth between text elements and whole texts (Palmer 1969). For example, reading the end paragraph of a story can illuminate a previous confusion or question about something near the beginning or reading something in another story can lead to a 'eureka' moment about another text read previously. At this point, probing questions began to be identified that could not be addressed using the text(s) alone. These were recorded to identify pertinent

material outside of the texts that could help in answering the questions arising (Prasad 2002).

- *Interpretation 4—Fusing*: this was about 'reading-in', where answers to the questions in Interpretation 3 were sought outside of the group of stories. This resulted in a fusion between: my social and cultural context through my critical engagement with research literature; the experiences in the stories and the experiences in evidence in other available stories (such as published accounts). I learnt from the stories and made connections between the documented experiences and a social psychological understanding of the society in which these stories exist (Alvesson and Sköldberg 2017; Gadamer and Linge 1976). At this point it was possible, and indeed desirable, that what I began to document was 'new', not necessarily just that which was included when the men wrote their story. Such insights may not have even been with me when I began work on the text but emerged as I interpreted the experiences. These new understandings may "... have come into being in and out of our engagement with it [the text]" (Crotty 1998: 110). (See Georgii-Hemming 2007 for further explication of this process of interpretation.)

Interpretative work was conducted iteratively, with Interpretation 4 of each story being written up for this book as 'The Story of....' It is hoped that this explanantion has been able to offer sufficient detail for another researcher to see my process in working with the texts. However, it should be noted that the nature of interpretative work means that there is not a rehearsed procedure to follow and much of the interpretative experience was immersive and relied primarily upon extensive re-reading of passages, texts and literature to produce the interpretations presented and discussed in the following chapters.

Reflexivity and Subjectivity

What qualitative interpretative psychology requires running through its core is a commitment to reflection and scrutiny of decisions and process- and findings-influences. This is especially true when the researcher needs to remain engaged with recognising their role in the research due to having personal experience of the topic under investigation. This can be termed reflexivity, which involves ongoing reflection through self-dialogue whilst living the experience of engaging in research. As Finlay and Gough (2003: 108) state:

> Reflexivity is thus the process of continually reflecting upon our interpretations of both our experience and the phenomena being studied so as to move beyond the partiality of our previous understandings and our investment in particular research outcomes.

Transparency in this process of interpretation, including my subjective experience, introspective analysis and critical insights were achieved through a commitment to journaling as a reflexive tool.

Journaling can allow the researcher to incorporate the research's impact on him and of he on the research, it can also help to guard against lapsing into merely anecdotal, protracted descriptive accounts rather than critically questioning. However, reflection carries with it a 'health warning' for the good of the finished research. It should not be a "…self-indulgent and reductive exercise that psychologizes phenomena and psychologizes your own part in producing them." (Parker 2005: 35). As seen in the quotation above, balance is key in avoiding the researcher's reflections drowning out the messages from the interpretative work. Part of this balance is asking the difficult questions about when self is encroaching upon the research, why that may be and what, if anything, needs to be done about it (Berg and Smith 1988). Alongside this, it is important to note that engaging in reflexive research will not somehow lead to my uncovering "'real' motivations" from within myself (Finlay and Gough 2003: 27). Reflexivity is necessarily incomplete and context-bound, I can only attend to experiential perceptions that occur as I research. This is why journaling feels quite so crucial; it at least provides a safe space for these questions and experiences to be worked out before inclusion in the finished write-up.

Being able to maintain a journal also allows for all of those integral, yet 'bitty' parts of the research experience that arise during the interpretative process that do not 'fit' into a linear format required of a book. The day-to-day questions, concerns, musings, ideas and personal responses need a conduit of some kind, rather than being allowed to form a soup in a researcher's mind. This is not just to enhance accountability through recording (Jasper 2005) but to externalise the extensive amount of thinking to give clarity, make connections, or to be legitimately discarded. At its simplest, hardback notebooks which could survive being carried around with me constantly were employed so that I could jot down reflections and realisations on-the-go. The scope of this journaling has been as extensive as the stories required: from issues with rendering particular phrases and meanings, to bigger understandings arrived at about the relationship between the stories and critical men's studies. They are a necessary record, given the interpretative principle that interpretation be as open as possible to permit the proliferation of alternative versions (McLeod 2001; Whitehead 2004).

If the premise is accepted that social reality is at once both objective and subjective (Georgii-Hemming 2007), the notion of subjectivity within research seems to be more problematic than that of objectivity (which tends to be a desired condition for the production of reliable knowledge), and so requires further exploration. This is a topic for which Parker (1997) has provided groundwork as he moved beyond a single notion of subjectivity. In his work three conceptualisations of subjectivity are discussed within the context of discursive psychology: blank, uncomplicated, and complex. It is the latter that is most useful to us here.

Parker (1997: 491) suggests a 'complex subjectivity':

> ...that takes seriously both the intentions and desires of the individual and the operation of social structures and discourse. A crucial part of this third notion of subjectivity, however, is that the cultural elements out of which a distinct sense of individuality are forged must be attended to.

This establishes subjectivity beyond the typical realm of the individual so central to the work of psychology, as it is able to incorporate the context in which the experiencer exists, both socially and culturally, viewing these as 'tangled' with the intentions of the individual. Subjectivity is presented as socially embedded but fragmented (Lupton 1997), as "...a constellation of dialogically structured subject positions enacted in the intersubjective space of the person's relations with others." (Georgaca 2001: 234). To the interpretative endeavour, however, it is the subjectivities to be found within text that are of interest because "the problem of subjectivity can only be solved when it is related to the problem of interpretation" (Levering 2006: 451). As it pertains to discourse analysis, which Parker develops, discourse alone is insufficient in the exploration of feeling and emotional experience (Burkitt 2002), especially when this experiential insight is shared through written text, separated over time and space from the original writer.

Within interpretative work the concept of subjectivity can be understood via the notion of a 'double hermeneutic': the text is the recording of the experiencer's meaning-making. This meaning-making contains a complex web of what the writer identifies as events, his personal experiences of himself, his thoughts, feelings and behaviours, along with his experience of others' interactions with him and responses to his disordered eating. This web is intricate and capable of expressing the writer's immediate experience of his past or present in the act of storytelling, as well as instances where he has held his experience up as an object to be re-examined and reflected upon.

In effect, the writer is the first interpreter, reading his account and deciding what belongs and what does not or deciding that what is in the text is enough as it stands. This involves reasoning and justifying on his part as he decides what constitutes a reliable, meaningful and real rendering of his experience for him to share. Some elements expressed within the story may be developed, while others may exist in the text unexplored; these may emerge later as questions posed by the researcher to the text or outside the text. The researcher's interpretation is thus the second pass at meaning-making where understanding of the experiencer's meaning-making is sought. This involves not only rendering an interpretation of the original story but an acceptance that interpretative work demands a commitment to "self-reflection as a precondition of successful interpretation." (Shalin 1986: 118).

I would add that, in addition, it could be said that there is a 'triple hermeneutic' taking place, as ultimately the reader makes meaning of the interpreting researcher's experience of the original interpreter's text. This is seen as a crucial part of circle of understanding: the interpretative act is not 'complete' until it is read (Alvesson and Sköldberg 2017). Therefore, in my research, there are several subjectivities enmeshed at once, making it multi-layered. This moves beyond complex subjectivity to what can be termed dynamic subjectivity, as each of the interpreters has their part to play in the process of understanding through the medium of text: with each new reader, a new interpretation comes into being. Each interpreter is unable to escape interpreting free of values or pre-judgements, and these are not formed isolated within the individual, as they are perceived through and shaped by the society that the interpreter belongs to.

References

Ahonen, P. S. (2003). *Men's Experience with Eating Disorders: Uncommon Lives? A Look at the Experiences of Men with Eating Disorders.* Chicago: Annual Conference of the American Educational Research Association.

Alvesson, M., & Sköldberg, K. (2009). *Reflexive Methodology: New Vistas for Qualitative Research.* London: SAGE Publications.

Alvesson, M., & Sköldberg, K. (2017). *Reflexive Methodology: New Vistas for Qualitative Research*. London: SAGE Publications.
American Psychiatric Association. (2013). *Diagnostic and Statistical Manual of Mental Disorders: Dsm-5*. Arlington, VA: American Psychiatric Association.
Andersen, A. E. (Ed.). (1985). *Practical Comprehensive Treatment of Anorexia Nervosa and Bulimia*. Baltimore, MD: Johns Hopkins University Press.
Andersen, A. E. (Ed.). (1990). *Males with Eating Disorders*. New York: Brunner/Mazel.
Andersen, A. E. (1995). Eating Disorders in Males. In K. D. Brownell & C. G. Fairburn (Eds.), *Eating Disorders and Obesity: A Comprehensive Handbook*. London: Guilford Press.
Andersen, A. E., & DiDomenico, L. (1992). Diet Vs. Shape Content of Popular Male and Female Magazines: A Dose-Response Relationship to the Incidence of Eating Disorders? *International Journal of Eating Disorders, 11*(3), 283–287.
Baghurst, T., Griffiths, S., & Murray, S. (2018). Boys and Girls Prefer Hyper-Muscular Male Action Figures over Normally-Muscular Action Figures: Evidence That Children Have Internalized the Muscular Male Body Ideal. *North American Journal of Psychology, 20*(1), 159–169.
Baghurst, T., Hollander, D. B., Nardella, B., & Haff, G. G. (2006). Change in Sociocultural Ideal Male Physique: An Examination of Past and Present Action Figures. *Body Image, 3*(1), 87–91.
Bartlett, B. A., & Mitchell, K. S. (2015). Eating Disorders in Military and Veteran Men and Women: A Systematic Review. *International Journal of Eating Disorders, 48*(8), 1057–1069.
Bayes, A., & Madden, S. (2011). Early Onset Eating Disorders in Male Adolescents: A Series of 10 Inpatients. *Australasian Psychiatry, 19*(6), 526–530.
Bénéï, V. (2011). Learning to Read? Hermeneutic Generosity and Productive Misreadings: A Response to Anthony Carter. *Journal of the Royal Anthropological Institute, 17*(4), 877–880.
Berg, D. N., & Smith, K. K. (1988). *The Self in Social Inquiry: Researching Methods*. Beverly Hills, CA: SAGE Publications.
Bernard, H. R. (2012). *Social Research Methods: Qualitative and Quantitative Approaches*. London: SAGE Publications.
Björk, T., Wallin, K., & Pettersen, G. (2012). Male Experiences of Life after Recovery from an Eating Disorder. *Eating Disorders, 20*(5), 460–468.
Blair, L., Aloia, C. R., Valliant, M. W., Knight, K. B., Garner, J. C., & Nahar, V. K. (2017). Association between Athletic Participation and the Risk of Eating Disorder and Body Dissatisfaction in College Students. *International Journal of Health Sciences, 11*(4), 8.
Boerner, L. M., Spillane, N. S., Anderson, K. G., & Smith, G. T. (2004). Similarities and Differences between Women and Men on Eating Disorder Risk Factors and Symptom Measures. *Eating Behaviors, 5*(3), 209–222.

Botha, D. (2012). *No Labels: Men in Relationship with Anorexia*. South Africa: Moonshine Media.

Brill, J. B., & Keane, M. W. (1994). Supplementation Patterns of Competitive Male and Female Bodybuilders. *International Journal of Sport Nutrition, 4*(4), 398–412.

Brooks, S. (1997). Anorexia: A Male Perspective. In R. Shelley (Ed.), *Anorexics on Anorexia* (pp. 53–60). London: Jessica Kingsley Publishers.

Bruni, F. (2009). *Born Round: The Secret History of a Full-Time Eater*. New York: Penguin Press.

Bryant-Jefferies, R. (2005). *Counselling for Eating Disorders in Men: Person-Centred Dialogues*. London: Radcliffe Publishing.

Burkitt, I. (2002). Complex Emotions: Relations, Feelings and Images in Emotional Experience. *The Sociological Review, 50*(S2), 151–167.

Burlew, L. D., & Shurts, W. M. (2013). Men and Body Image: Current Issues and Counseling Implications. *Journal of Counseling & Development, 91*(4), 428–435.

Burr, V. (2015). *Social Constructionism*. Hove: Routledge.

Campling, M. (2007). A Person-Centred Response to Eating Disorders: A Personal Experience. In R. Worsley & S. Joseph (Eds.), *Person-Centred Practice: Case Studies in Positive Psychology*. Ross-on-Wye: PCCS Books.

Campling, M. (2012). *The Nature of Anorexia and Recovery: A Heuristic Self-Search Inquiry*. (pp. 127). London: University of Wales.

Cohn, L., & Lemberg, R. (Eds.). (2014). *Current Findings on Males with Eating Disorders*. Hove: Routledge.

Compte, E. J., Sepúlveda, A. R., & Torrente, F. (2018). Approximations to an Integrated Model of Eating Disorders and Muscle Dysmorphia among University Male Students in Argentina. *Men and Masculinities*. https://doi.org/10.1177/1097184X17753039.

Corson, P. W., & Andersen, A. E. (2002). Body Image Issues among Boys and Men. In T. F. Cash & T. Pruzinsky (Eds.), *Body Image: A Handbook of Theory, Research, and Clinical Practice* (pp. 192–199). New York: Guilford Press.

Costin, C. (2007). *Eating Disorder Sourcebook*. New York: McGraw-Hill.

Crotty, M. (1998). *The Foundations of Social Research: Meaning and Perspective in the Research Process*. London: SAGE Publications.

Cuban, B. (2013). *Shattered Image: My Triumph over Body Dysmorphic Disorder*. Canyon Country, CA: NetMinds.

Dakanalis, A., & Riva, G. (2013). Current Considerations for Eating and Body-Related Disorders among Men. In L. B. Sams & J. A. Keel (Eds.), *Handbook on Body Image: Gender Differences, Sociocultural Influences and Health Implications* (pp. 195–216). New York: Nova Science Publications.

Dalgliesh, J., & Nutt, K. (2013). Treating Men with Eating Disorders in the NHS. *Nursing Standard, 27*(35), 42–46.

Darcy, A. M. (2011). Eating Disorders in Adolescent Males: A Critical Examination of Five Common Assumptions. *Adolescent Psychiatry, 1*(4), 307–312.

Davis, C., & Scott-Robertson, L. (2000). A Psychological Comparison of Females with Anorexia Nervosa and Competitive Male Bodybuilders: Body Shape Ideals in the Extreme. *Eating Behaviors, 1*(1), 33–46.

Delderfield, R. (2013, March). Coming out of the Food Cupboard: Supporting Young Men with Eating Disorders. *University and College Counselling Journal, 2013*(2), 13–15.

Delderfield, R. (2014, April 8). Men Get Eating Disorders Too…And Often Can't Talk About Them. *The Conversation*, pp. 1–2.

Denscombe, M. (2010). *Ground Rules for Social Research: Guidelines for Good Practice*. Maidenhead: McGraw-Hill Education.

Devrim, A., Bilgic, P., & Hongu, N. (2018). Is There Any Relationship between Body Image Perception, Eating Disorders, and Muscle Dysmorphic Disorders in Male Bodybuilders? *American Journal of Men's Health, 12*(5), 1746–1758.

Elliott, J. (2005). *Using Narrative in Social Research: Qualitative and Quantitative Approaches*. SAGE Publications.

Ellis, C., Kiesinger, C. E., & Tillmann-Healy, L. M. (1997). Interactive Interviewing: Talking About Emotional Experience. In R. Hertz (Ed.), *Reflexivity and Voice* (pp. 119–149). London: SAGE Publications.

Essayli, J. H., Murakami, J. M., & Latner, J. D. (2018). Perceived Sexual Orientation of Men and Women with Eating Disorders and Obesity. *Journal of Homosexuality* (just-accepted) https://doiorg.brad.idm.oclc.org/10.1080/00918369.2018.1484228.

Evans, J. (2011). *Becoming John: Anorexia's Not Just for Girls*. Didcot: Xlibris.

Fay, B. (1996). *Contemporary Philosophy of Social Science: A Multicultural Approach*. Cambridge: Cambridge University Press.

Feltman, K. A., & Ferraro, F. R. (2011). Preliminary Data on Risk Factors and Disordered Eating in Male College Students. *Current Psychology, 30*(2), 194–202.

Finlay, L., & Gough, B. (Eds.). (2003). *Reflexivity: A Practical Guide for Researchers in Health and Social Sciences*. Oxford: John Wiley & Sons.

Forbush, K. T., Wildes, J. E., & Hunt, T. K. (2014). Gender Norms, Psychometric Properties, and Validity for the Eating Pathology Symptoms Inventory. *International Journal of Eating Disorders, 47*(1), 85–91.

Forney, K. J., Holland, L. A., & Keel, P. K. (2012). Influence of Peer Context on the Relationship between Body Dissatisfaction and Eating Pathology in Women and Men. *International Journal of Eating Disorders, 45*(8), 982–989.

Gadamer, H. G., & Linge, D. E. (1976). *Philosophical Hermeneutics*. Berkeley, CA: University of California Press.

Georgaca, E. (2001). Voices of the Self in Psychotherapy: A Qualitative Analysis. *British Journal of Medical Psychology, 74*(2), 223–236.

Georgii-Hemming, E. (2007). Hermeneutic Knowledge: Dialogue between Experiences. *Research Studies in Music Education, 29*(1), 13–28.
Gila, A., Castro, J., Cesena, J., & Toro, J. (2005). Anorexia Nervosa in Male Adolescents: Body Image, Eating Attitudes and Psychological Traits. *The Journal of Adolescent Health, 36*(3), 221–226.
Gilmore, D. D. (1994). The Beauty of the Beast: Male Body Imagery in Anthropological Perspective. In M. G. Winkler & L. B. Cole (Eds.), *The Good Body: Asceticism in Contemporary Culture* (pp. 191–214). Oxford: Berghahn Books.
Good, G. E., & Wood, P. K. (1995). Male Gender Role Conflict, Depression, and Help Seeking: Do College Men Face Double Jeopardy? *Journal of Counseling & Development, 74*(1), 70–75.
Grahl, G. A. (2007). *Skinny Boy: A Young Man's Battle and Triumph over Anorexia*. Clearfield, UT: American Legacy.
Greenberg, S. T., & Schoen, E. G. (2008). Males and Eating Disorders: Gender-Based Therapy for Eating Disorder Recovery. *Professional Psychology: Research and Practice, 39*(4), 464.
Grieve, F. G. (2007). A Conceptual Model of Factors Contributing to the Development of Muscle Dysmorphia. *Eating Behaviors, 15*(1), 63–80.
Griffiths, S., Mond, J. M., Li, Z., Gunatilake, S., Murray, S. B., Sheffield, J., & Touyz, S. (2015). Self-Stigma of Seeking Treatment and Being Male Predict an Increased Likelihood of Having an Undiagnosed Eating Disorder. *International Journal of Eating Disorders, 48*(6), 775–778.
Griffiths, S., Mond, J. M., Murray, S. B., & Touyz, S. (2013). Young Peoples' Stigmatizing Attitudes and Beliefs About Anorexia Nervosa and Muscle Dysmorphia. *International Journal of Eating Disorders, 47*(2), 189–195.
Griffiths, S., Murray, S. B., Krug, I., & McLean, S. A. (2018). The Contribution of Social Media to Body Dissatisfaction, Eating Disorder Symptoms, and Anabolic Steroid Use among Sexual Minority Men. *Cyberpsychology, Behavior, and Social Networking, 21*(3), 149–156.
Gueguen, J., Godart, N., Chambry, J., Brun-Eberentz, A., Foulon, C., Divac Phd, S. M., Guelfi, J. D., Rouillon, F., Falissard, B., & Huas, C. (2012). Severe Anorexia Nervosa in Men: Comparison with Severe an in Women and Analysis of Mortality. *International Journal of Eating Disorders, 45*(4), 537–545.
Halperin, E. N. (1996). The Role of Socialization in Male Anorexia Nervosa: Two Cases. *Child Psychiatry and Human Development, 26*(3), 159–168.
Harvey, J. A., & Robinson, J. D. (2003). Eating Disorders in Men: Current Considerations. *Journal of Clinical Psychology in Medical Settings, 10*(4), 297–306.
Hesse-Biber, S. J. (1996). *Am I Thin Enough Yet?: The Cult of Thinness and the Commercialization of Identity*. Oxford: Oxford University Press.

Holbrook, T. (2000). Walking in the Woods. In A. E. Andersen, L. Cohn, & T. Holbrook (Eds.), *Making Weight: Men's Conflicts with Food, Weight, Shape & Appearance* (pp. 117–134). Carlsbad, CA: Gürze Books.

Jasper, M. A. (2005). Using Reflective Writing within Research. *Journal of Research in Nursing, 10*(3), 247–260.

Jones, W. R., & Morgan, J. F. (2010). Eating Disorders in Men: A Review of the Literature. *Journal of Public Mental Health, 9*(2), 23–31.

Karimian, J., & Esfahani, P. S. (2011). Supplement Consumption in Body Builder Athletes. *Journal of Research in Medical Sciences, 16*(10), 1347–1353.

Kelly, N. R., Cotter, E., & Guidinger, C. (2018). Men Who Engage in Both Subjective and Objective Binge Eating Have the Highest Psychological and Medical Comorbidities. *Eating Behaviors, 30*, 115–119.

Kinnaird, E., Norton, C., & Tchanturia, K. (2018). Clinicians' Views on Treatment Adaptations for Men with Eating Disorders: A Qualitative Study. *BMJ Open, 8*(8), e021934.

Kohl, J. (2009). *Skeletal Marriage.* San Jose, CA: CreateSpace.

Krasnow, M. (1996). *My Life as a Male Anorexic.* New York: Harrington Park Press.

Lantz, C. D., Rhea, D. J., & Cornelius, A. E. (2002). Muscle Dysmorphia in Elite-Level Power Lifters and Bodybuilders: A Test of Differences within a Conceptual Model. *The Journal of Strength & Conditioning Research, 16*(4), 649–655.

Leith, W. (2010). *The Hungry Years: Confessions of a Food Addict.* Toronto: Anchor Canada.

LeVasseur, J. J. (2003). The Problem of Bracketing in Phenomenology. *Qualitative Health Research, 13*(3), 408–420.

Levering, B. (2006). Epistemological Issues in Phenomenological Research: How Authoritative Are People's Accounts of Their Own Perceptions? *Journal of Philosophy of Education, 40*(4), 451–462.

Lock, J. D. (2009). Trying to Fit Square Pegs in Round Holes: Eating Disorders in Males. *The Journal of Adolescent Health, 44*(2), 99–100.

Lupton, D. (1997). Consumerism, Reflexivity and the Medical Encounter. *Social Science & Medicine, 45*(3), 373–381.

MacCaughelty, C., Wagner, R., & Rufino, K. (2016). Does Being Overweight or Male Increase a Patient's Risk of Not Being Referred for an Eating Disorder Consult? *International Journal of Eating Disorders, 49*(10), 963–966.

Maine, M., & Bunnell, D. (2008). How Do the Principles of the Feminist, Relational Model Apply to Treatment of Men with Eating Disorders and Related Issues? *Eating Behaviors, 16*(2), 187–192.

Marshall, C., & Rossman, G. B. (2011). *Designing Qualitative Research.* London: SAGE Publications.

Mauthner, N., & Doucet, A. (1998). Reflections on a Voice-Centred Relational Method. In J. Ribbens & R. Edwards (Eds.), *Feminist Dilemmas in Qualitative*

Research: Public Knowledge and Private Lives (pp. 119–146). London: SAGE Publications.

McBride, G. (2014). *Weightless: My Life as a Fat Man and How I Escaped.* New York: Central Recovery Press, LLC.

McCabe, M., & Ricciardelli, L. (2004). Weight and Shape Concerns of Boys and Men. In J. K. Thompson (Ed.), *Handbook of Eating Disorders and Obesity* (pp. 606–634). New York: Wiley.

McLean, S. A., Paxton, S. J., Massey, R., Hay, P. J., Mond, J. M., & Rodgers, B. (2014). Stigmatizing Attitudes and Beliefs About Bulimia Nervosa: Gender, Age, Education and Income Variability in a Community Sample. *International Journal of Eating Disorders, 47*(4), 353–361.

McLeod, J. (2001). *Qualitative Research in Counselling and Psychotherapy.* London: SAGE Publications.

McLeod, J. (2010). *Case Study Research in Counselling and Psychotherapy.* London: SAGE Publications.

Mehler, P. S., & Andersen, A. E. (2017). *Eating Disorders: A Guide to Medical Care and Complications.* Baltimore, MD: Johns Hopkins University Press.

Mehler, P. S., Blalock, D. V., Walden, K., Kaur, S., McBride, J., Walsh, K., & Watts, J. (2018). Medical Findings in 1,026 Consecutive Adult Inpatient–Residential Eating Disordered Patients. *International Journal of Eating Disorders, 51*(4), 305–313.

Mitchell, J. E., Agras, S., Crow, S., Halmi, K., Fairburn, C. G., Bryson, S., & Kraemer, H. (2011). Stepped Care and Cognitive-Behavioural Therapy for Bulimia Nervosa: Randomised Trial. *British Journal of Psychiatry, 198*(5), 391–397.

Mitchell, L., Murray, S. B., Hoon, M., Hackett, D., Prvan, T., & O'Connor, H. (2017). Correlates of Muscle Dysmorphia Symptomatology in Natural Bodybuilders: Distinguishing Factors in the Pursuit of Hyper-Muscularity. *Body image, 22*, 1–5.

Mitchison, D., Mond, J., Slewa-Younan, S., & Hay, P. (2013). Sex Differences in Health-Related Quality of Life Impairment Associated with Eating Disorder Features: A General Population Study. *International Journal of Eating Disorders, 46*(4), 375–380.

Morgan, J. F. (2000). From Charles Atlas to Adonis Complex—Fat Is More than a Feminist Issue. *The Lancet, 356*(9239), 1372–1373.

Morgan, J. F. (2013). Male Eating Disorders. In J. Alexander & J. Treasure (Eds.), *A Collaborative Approach to Eating Disorders.* London: Routledge.

Morgan, J. F., & Arcelus, J. (2009). Body Image in Gay and Straight Men: A Qualitative Study. *European Eating Disorders Review, 17*(6), 435–443.

Mosley, P. E. (2009). Bigorexia: Bodybuilding and Muscle Dysmorphia. *European Eating Disorders Review, 17*(3), 191–198.

Muise, A. M., Stein, D. G., & Arbess, G. (2003). Eating Disorders in Adolescent Boys: A Review of the Adolescent and Young Adult Literature. *Journal of Adolescent Health, 33*(6), 427–435.

Murphy-Robinson, M. (2007). Men Don't Get Anorexia, Do They? *Openmind, 144*, 16–17.

Murray, S. B., Griffiths, S., & Mond, J. M. (2016). Evolving Eating Disorder Psychopathology: Conceptualising Muscularity-Oriented Disordered Eating. *The British Journal of Psychiatry, 208*(5), 414–415.

Murray, S. B., Nagata, J. M., Griffiths, S., Calzo, J. P., Brown, T. A., Mitchison, D., Blashill, A. J., & Mond, J. M. (2017). The Enigma of Male Eating Disorders: A Critical Review and Synthesis. *Clinical Psychology Review, 57*, 1–11.

Murray, S. B., Rieger, E., Touyz, S. W., & De la Garza Garcia Lic, Y. (2010). Muscle Dysmorphia and the Dsm-V Conundrum: Where Does It Belong? A Review Paper. *International Journal of Eating Disorders, 43*(6), 483–491.

Newton, B. J., Rothlingova, Z., Gutteridge, R., LeMarchand, K., & Raphael, J. H. (2012). No Room for Reflexivity? Critical Reflections Following a Systematic Review of Qualitative Research. *Journal of Health Psychology, 17*(6), 866–885.

Nolan, J. (2008). Hungry Men. In K. Taylor (Ed.), *Going Hungry: Writers on Desire, Self-Denial, and Overcoming Anorexia* (pp. 69–88). New York: Anchor Books.

Núñez-Navarro, A., Agüera, Z., Krug, I., Jiménez-Murcia, S., Sánchez, I., Araguz, N., Gorwood, P., Granero, R., Penelo, E., Karwautz, A., Moragas, L., Saldaña, S., Treasure, J., Menchón, J. M., & Fernández-Aranda, F. (2012). Do Men with Eating Disorders Differ from Women in Clinics, Psychopathology and Personality? *European Eating Disorders Review, 20*(1), 23–31.

O'Dea, J. A., & Abraham, S. (2002). Eating and Exercise Disorders in Young College Men. *Journal of American College Health, 50*(6), 273–278.

Olivardia, R. (2002). Body Image and Muscularity. In F. T. Cash & T. Pruzinsky (Eds.), *Body Image: A Handbook of Theory, Research, and Clinical Practice* (pp. 210–218). New York: Guilford Press.

Palmer, R. E. (1969). *Hermeneutics: Interpretation Theory in Schleiermacher, Dilthey, Heidegger, and Gadamer*. Evanston, IL: Northwestern University Press.

Parker, I. (1997). Discourse Analysis and Psychoanalysis. *British Journal of Social Psychology, 36*(4), 479–495.

Parker, I. (2005). *Qualitative Psychology: Introducing Radical Research*. Maidenhead: Open University Press.

Peixoto Labre, M. (2002). Adolescent Boys and the Muscular Male Body Ideal. *Journal of Adolescent Health, 30*(4), 233–242.

Pettersen, G., Wallin, K., & Björk, T. (2016). How Do Males Recover from Eating Disorders? An Interview Study. *BMJ Open, 6*(8), e010760.

Pope, C. G., Pope, H. G., Menard, W., Fay, C., Olivardia, R., & Phillips, K. A. (2005). Clinical Features of Muscle Dysmorphia among Males with Body Dysmorphic Disorder. *Body Image, 2*(4), 395–400.

Pope, H., Phillips, K. A., & Olivardia, R. (2000). *The Adonis Complex: The Secret Crisis of Male Body Obsession*. New York: Simon and Schuster.

Pope Jr., H. G., Gruber, A. J., Choi, P., Olivardia, R., & Phillips, K. A. (1997). Muscle Dysmorphia: An Underrecognized Form of Body Dysmorphic Disorder. *Psychosomatics, 38*(6), 548–557.

Pope, H. G., Katz, D. L., & Hudson, J. I. (1993). Anorexia Nervosa and "Reverse Anorexia" among 108 Male Bodybuilders. *Comprehensive Psychiatry, 34*(6), 406–409.

Prager, M. (2010). *Fat Boy Thin Man*. Los Gatos, CA: Smashwords.

Prasad, A. (2002). The Contest over Meaning: Hermeneutics as an Interpretive Methodology for Understanding Texts. *Organizational Research Methods, 5*(1), 12–33.

Raevuori, A., Keski-Rahkonen, A., Hoek, H. W., Sihvola, E., Rissanen, A., & Kaprio, J. (2008). Lifetime Anorexia Nervosa in Young Men in the Community: Five Cases and Their Co-Twins. *International Journal of Eating Disorders, 41*(5), 458–463.

Räisänen, U., & Hunt, K. (2014). The Role of Gendered Constructions of Eating Disorders in Delayed Help-Seeking in Men: A Qualitative Interview Study. *BMJ Open, 4*(4), 1–8.

Ray, S. L. (2004). Eating Disorders in Adolescent Males. *Professional School Counseling, 8*(2), 98–101.

Robinson, K. J., Mountford, V. A., & Sperlinger, D. J. (2013). Being Men with Eating Disorders: Perspectives of Male Eating Disorder Service-Users. *Journal of Health Psychology, 18*(2), 176–186.

Rodgers, R. F., Ganchou, C., Franko, D. L., & Chabrol, H. (2012). Drive for Muscularity and Disordered Eating among French Adolescent Boys: A Sociocultural Model. *Body Image, 9*(3), 318–323.

Ruiz, R. (2008). The Ghost of Gordolfo Gelatino. In K. Taylor (Ed.), *Going Hungry: Writers on Desire, Self-Denial, and Overcoming Anorexia* (pp. 149–166). New York: Anchor Books.

Russell, L., & Laszlo, B. (2013). A Group for Men with Eating Disorders: When "Lone Wolves" Come Together. *Men and Masculinities, 16*(2), 252–259.

Samuel, D. G. (2008). The Tale of an Anorexic Male Medical Student. *British Medical Journal, 336*(7649), 892–892.

Saxen, R. (2007). *The Good Eater: The True Story of One Man's Struggle with Binge Eating Disorder*. Oakland, CA: New Harbinger.

Schleiermacher, F., & Bowie, A. (1998). *Schleiermacher: Hermeneutics and Criticism: And Other Writings*. Cambridge: Cambridge University Press.

Shalin, D. N. (1986). Romanticism and the Rise of Sociological Hermeneutics. *Social Research, 53*(1), 77–123.

Shaughnessy, J. J., & Zechmeister, E. B. (2006). *Research Methods in Psychology.* New York: Alfred A. Knopf.

Shingleton, R. M., Thompson-Brenner, H., Thompson, D. R., Pratt, E. M., & Franko, D. L. (2015). Gender Differences in Clinical Trials of Binge Eating Disorder: An Analysis of Aggregated Data. *Journal of Consulting and Clinical Psychology, 83*(2), 382–386.

Silverman, D. (2005). *Doing Qualitative Research: A Practical Handbook.* London: SAGE Publications.

Silverman, D. (2006). *Interpreting Qualitative Data.* London: SAGE Publications.

Simon, S. (2006). *Male Bulimia: My Dark Demon.* Lincoln, NE: iUniverse.

Smart, R. (2006). A Man with a "Woman's Problem": Male Gender and Eating Disorders. In M. Englar-Carlson & M. A. Stevens (Eds.), *In the Room with Men: A Casebook of Therapeutic Change* (pp. 319–338). Washington, DC: American Psychological Association.

Smink, F. R., Van Hoeken, D., & Hoek, H. W. (2012). Epidemiology of Eating Disorders: Incidence, Prevalence and Mortality Rates. *Current Psychiatry Reports, 14*(4), 406–414.

Smink, F. R., van Hoeken, D., Oldehinkel, A. J., & Hoek, H. W. (2014). Prevalence and Severity of Dsm-5 Eating Disorders in a Community Cohort of Adolescents. *International Journal of Eating Disorders, 47*(6), 610–619.

Smith, J. A. (Ed.). (2008). *Qualitative Psychology: A Practical Guide to Research Methods.* London: SAGE Publications.

Støving, R. K., Andries, A., Brixen, K., Bilenberg, N., & Horder, K. (2011). Gender Differences in Outcome of Eating Disorders: A Retrospective Cohort Study. *Psychiatry Research, 186*(2), 362–366.

Striegel, R. H., Bedrosian, R., Wang, C., & Schwartz, S. (2012). Why Men Should Be Included in Research on Binge Eating: Results from a Comparison of Psychosocial Impairment in Men and Women. *International Journal of Eating Disorders, 45*(2), 233–240.

Sweeting, H., Walker, L., Maclean, A. M., Patterson, C., & Räisänen, U. (2015). Prevalence of Eating Disorders in Males: A Review of Rates Reported in Academic Research and UK Mass Media. *International Journal of Men's Health, 14*(2), 86–112.

Till, C. (2011). The Quantification of Gender: Anorexia Nervosa and Femininity. *Health Sociology Review, 20*(4), 437–449.

Turel, T., Jameson, M., Gitimu, P., Rowlands, Z., Mincher, J., & Pohle-Krauza, R. (2018). Disordered Eating: Influence of Body Image, Sociocultural Attitudes, Appearance Anxiety and Depression-a Focus on College Males and a Gender Comparison. *Cogent Psychology*, 1483062.

Turja, T., Oksanen, A., Kaakinen, M., Sirola, A., Kaltiala-Heino, R., & Räsänen, P. (2017). Proeating Disorder Websites and Subjective Well-Being: A Four-Country Study on Young People. *International Journal of Eating Disorders, 50*(1), 50–57.

Tylka, T. L., & Subich, L. M. (2002). A Preliminary Investigation of the Eating Disorder Continuum with Men. *Journal of Counseling Psychology, 49*(2), 273–279.

Whitehead, L. (2004). Enhancing the Quality of Hermeneutic Research: Decision Trail. *Journal of Advanced Nursing, 45*(5), 512–518.

Wilkinson, D. (2002). *The Researcher's Toolkit: The Complete Guide to Practitioner Research.* London: Routledge.

Wilps, R. F. (1990). Male Bulimia Nervosa: An Autobiographical Case Study. In A. E. Andersen (Ed.), *Males with Eating Disorders* (pp. 9–29). New York: Brunner/Mazel.

Wortham, S. (2000). Interactional Positioning and Narrative Self-Construction. *Narrative Inquiry, 10*(1), 157–184.

Wright, J., Halse, C., & Levy, G. (2016). Preteen Boys, Body Image, and Eating Disorders. *Men and Masculinities, 19*(1), 3–21.

CHAPTER 2

Stoicism and Fugliness

Abstract One man's experiences with trauma through fraternal suicide, violence, homelessness, and self-loathing are analysed. Bingeing and purging using laxatives and other compensatory behaviours are discussed. The concept of stoic masculinity in male eating disorders is presented and debated in light of this man's willingness to seek help. The idea of recovery appears but this is contrasted with a continued use of dieting. 'Fugliness' is introduced, explained and discussed.

Keywords Stoic masculinity • Fugly • Bingeing and purging • Suicide • Male dieting

The interpretative work begins here. To achieve consistency a similar pattern has been maintained in each substantive chapter, with the exception of this preamble. I begin with a critical interpretation that is informed and supported by extracts from the man's original story. Extracts may be contracted but otherwise, they are unchanged, hence, any idiosyncratic grammatical/spelling peculiarities. A discussion section follows. This elicits significant points that arise from the interpretation to explore and elucidate new understanding. Any demographic detail appearing (see previous chapter) is only that which could be gleaned from the volunteered story.

R. Delderfield, *Male Eating Disorders*,
https://doi.org/10.1007/978-3-030-02535-9_2

Anything outside of the story was not requested. Josh shared that he was 31 years old at the time of his contribution. He is not originally from Yorkshire but his story suggests that he may have been resident here at the time of writing.

The Story of Josh

Josh's feeling of being overweight is historical, something that can easily be traced back to his childhood; he is not alone as other men have distinct memories of being overweight as a child prior to the development of a difficult relationship with food, and this tends to be a feature within men who develop disordered eating more so than women (Cohn and Lemberg 2014; Gueguen et al. 2012; Strother et al. 2012; Strumia 2011). Other men's stories also reflect this (Bruni 2009; Prager 2010), having early years marred by how much heavier than other children they were. Josh terms himself as a chubby child but he points out other children did not tend to use such mild words. Instead, far crueller names were used, such as fat. Derogatory terms, like 'fat', mark out appearance as being the focal point of bullying and this known to lead to the development of future unhealthy attitudes towards weight as an adult (Madowitz et al. 2012; White et al. 2018). The early links between being aware of weight and the way others made us feel about it, is something that is felt to be at the core of some men's relationship with food (see the next chapter).

We Are Only as Sick as Our Secrets

Being aware of his overweight and the subsequent bullying this incurred was not the only early experience of significance. When Josh was only fourteen, his elder brother committed suicide, which is an exceedingly distressing thing to happen to anyone, let alone a teenager who is just maturing into how to handle life.

> I was only 14 and no one knew this was coming; he fought a very private battle with depression. His diary, his suicide letter, told the full story. He was also quite large as are many in our family. He started a diet leading up to his death and stopped eating chocolate. In fact on the envelope containing his suicide letter he wrote "p.s. still haven't eaten any chocolate". I think it's fair to say my brother had his own battles with eating.

The fact that he relates this as being without any warning signs adds to the tragic nature of this life event. There are no unequivocal data that prove what causes someone to turn specifically to food as a coping mechanism following such difficult times (Culbert et al. 2015). The loss of his brother is something that featured heavily in the remainder of Josh's experiences, as his suicide is used as a time milestone, in relation to which other momentous things take place. His brother had managed to keep his severe problems secret, internalised, and only when he was gone did Josh's family find out the full truth, including the extent of his struggle with depression. The power of remaining silent on our internal struggles is captured deftly by Michael Prager (2010: 103): "we're only as sick as our secrets." In which case, Josh's brother felt extremely unwell indeed and faced his struggle alone for so long.

His brother chose to give up eating a specific food that had seemed to take on a larger meaning for him. This foodstuff even featured on the envelope of the letter he left behind following his suicide: alongside a decision to end his own life, his 'parting shot' was that he had kept to his promise to cut out eating chocolate. This represents a painfully mundane observation to the family who dealt with his death but demonstrates the enormous importance of a food as a dangerous enemy for Josh's brother, as well as being notable to Josh himself. He made the connection that his brother had had a lonely and tragic relationship with something that other people find so inconsequential—food. Josh does not particularly further identify whether he discovered that there were other contributory factors that fed into his brother's depression, despite his family reading the journal that his brother left behind.

Some of his brother's personal struggles would come to foreshadow his own. His brother was heavier built, which is a family trait. This is something that other stories also include (Bruni 2009) with reference to how they were fed, not just how hereditary physiology developed as they grew up. As such, Josh's relationship with food was at least partly influenced by his family life, if not a direct result of him emulating his brother in particular. He clearly attributes his brother's death as the beginning of his own depression, something that he still feels and that he thinks is unlikely to end:

> His death started a 17 year battle with depression that I am still fighting and think I always will be.

This spiral into negative emotions which then manifest as disordered eating as a result of a single significant trauma is apparent elsewhere in men's experiences (see Chap. 5 where Richard's parents' marital breakdown began his experience with extreme restricting then bingeing). However, looking for a unified identifiable 'trigger' of different eating disorders has proved problematic (Birmingham et al. 2009) and rather than a single factor, disordered eating in men is perceived to develop multi-factorially in 'stages' (Andersen 1990). If the experience of his brother alone had not been enough to make him psychologically reach for a way to cope, what followed certainly would.

One Thing After Another

Very destructive life experiences happened to Josh in what appears to be a relatively short space of time. These included: losing his family unit as it fragmented; moving somewhere different to live apart from his family; losing someone dear to him when his relationship with his girlfriend ended; someone trying to kill him and attempting to end his own life as his depression deepened.

> Four years after his death I found myself living in a different town after the complete break up of my family, my own suicide attempt, a serious relationship with a girl that had ended, someone attempting to murder me and homelessness. It's fair to say those were exceptionally difficult times.

Some of the life experiences that Josh has endured have been shown to precede the onset of disordered eating (Pike et al. 2006). Two years later, he went on to be beaten by a member of his family. Often in eating disorders sexual abuse is particularly emphasised as a risk factor, however, in Josh's experience the abuse suffered was physical. Being exposed to violence is something that appears as a feature of male bulimia sufferers' history (Mitchell et al. 2011) and following assault, traumatic stress can lead to the development of disordered eating (Dubosc et al. 2012; Witte et al. 2012). After this, he ended up living on the streets. This calls to mind the idea of 'the body as the scene of the crime' where Josh's own physicality represents the site at which all of these violations took place (Frank 1995). Experiencing such close-to-home bodily traumatic events can result in a compounding of destructive emotional states that lead to hopelessness, which in turn can lead to the contemplation of suicide (Bureau et al.

2012). Josh eventually tried to commit suicide and perhaps this is unsurprising: he desperately wanted to exercise some control over his life and eliminate years of pain (Kingerlee 2012) and there is some suggestion that imitating suicidal behaviour does occur within families (Mann 2002).

Josh presents these events as a 'roll-call', given as an understated list that does not reflect the level of upheaval, distress and trauma that these evoke. This may belie Josh having made sense of this litany by reducing it to the status of a factual, emotionless set of discrete events without recourse to further exploration of what he went through. Despite men consciously recording their experiences as a story, the gendered nature of emotional expression suggests that full emotive exploration of all of the events that happened to Josh is unlikely to occur (Gough 2018). Stoical masculinity compounds (Ridge et al. 2011) a feature of those who experience disordered eating: they struggle to verbally identify and articulate emotions (Nowakowski et al. 2013). Josh avoids evoking unnecessary pain when telling his story, which remains undetailed. This is echoed when men are brought together to talk about their painful psychological experiences around eating, even in a supportive environment (Russell and Laszlo 2013).

Purging as Punishment

This is the background to his disordered eating's presentation, it grew under extremely adverse circumstances. Josh's first experiences in managing his weight were physically punishing, a method that seems more like mediaeval torture: taking scalding hot baths as an antidote to his weight, hoping calories would be burnt off.

> It was at this time I experienced the physical happening of my own eating disorder. Scalding hot baths in the belief that somehow I would lose weight as a consequence was an early manifestation, stupid in hindsight. I bought a bottle of laxatives. I took one and nothing happened. I took more and nothing happened. I chose to go for a walk, I was feeling really down and depressed. Whilst out walking something did happen. I was far from anywhere and the next two hours were two of the most shameful of my life.

The physical manifestation of his eating problems seems to feel separate to the psychological aspects. Perhaps this is because his negative relationship with food already existed psychologically long before he began purging and bingeing. These behaviours represented the emergence of his relationship with his body and weight. Josh himself draws no specific conclusion about why the effects of all these personal difficulties were directed at weight-loss, but his early experience of being chubby suggests the creation of a negative relationship between his body-in-the-world and his suffering at the hands of others. Contributing to this is a lack of resources, which meant his inward-focused punishment was exacted bodily because he did not have money or independent circumstances that might have led to other options being available, such as abuse of illegal drugs or gambling. He describes this as an exceptionally difficult time. Perhaps it was the case of only being able to handle so much stress, aggression and suffering before the dam broke and the disordered eating emerged, under its guise of helping him through (Campling 2012).

He tried using laxatives but in an early experimental episode, and desperate to feel the effect, Josh took large amounts in such short succession only for him to experience no effect. Following which he felt low as his method had not worked. Josh walked and walked, at which time the laxatives then took effect in a deeply unpleasant and inopportune moment and he still feels the shame to this day. There appears to have been little awareness of the way laxatives worked and yet he had been able to get hold of so many of them and clearly expected something more from their effects than simply the delayed sensation of emptiness following evacuation. This accords with another man's experience of laxative abuse. Frank Bruni (2009) says he operated on the premise that using laxatives would at least make him feel thinner, and possibly make him look slimmer, even though he has now learnt that is untrue.

Nevertheless, such a shameful, painful experience did not deter further experimentation with laxative medications. Approximately six years on since his brother's death things were becoming steadily worse. He seems to put the eating issues and depression hand-in-hand by this point. Family problems arose again for Josh when he was physically assaulted.

> I found myself homeless again, leaving my house in fear of further violence. I arrived in Yorkshire with just a bag of clothes and a little money. It was in 1999 my doctor referred me to the eating disorder clinic in Leeds. I had continued experimenting with laxatives and anything else I could obtain to try and purge myself of food. Drinking concoctions of liver salts to attempt to purge myself, the mix so strong the fluid burnt. Attempting to make myself sick any which way possible. Laxatives became my drug of choice, by the handful.

This was the point Josh mentions in his list, when he was intensely beaten by a family member. Being under attack and physically abused has emerged in other stories; Gareth suffered being punched and kicked (see Chap. 3). As a result, Josh became homeless once again, escaping to avoid any more abuse. He moved to another town but with no money and just a bag of clothes. This suggests that this was a highly destabilising move. Instability brings with it a significant level of uncertainty, potentially living hour-to-hour, let alone day-to-day. Living in a state of uncertainty is something that has been found to be specific to people with bingeing and purging (Frank et al. 2012), which Josh's experience seems to bear out. Other men's stories do not show that they struggled with periods of homelessness and this is not an experience I have had myself. It is difficult to perceive of the uncertainty, loneliness and fear this involves, let alone its contribution to impaired mental health.

Once he had moved to West Yorkshire, by the end of the 90s, Josh was finally sent not just for help, but highly-specialised help. His purging had taken on seriously invasive methods, including further experimentation with laxatives and use of strong liver salts solutions. There feels as if there were a desperation to find something, anything, that would work, enduring the burning sensation and pain in the pursuit of ridding his body, which began to include trying to vomit. The theme of punishing the body does arise in disordered eating (Chan et al. 2013; Williamson and Hartley 1998), though not as often as I had thought, yet the caustic action of dosing up on liver salts seems redolent of this. Taking liver salts (laxatives of any sort, really) can be exhausting and damaging to the body through severe electrolyte disturbance (Fairburn and Harrison 2003). It seems as if it took trial and error to get the purging 'right', this certainly reflects my own experiences, where it took real work to find the 'best' way to purge for maximum effect.

Bingeing Tightens Its Grip

Despite getting initial treatment relatively early on, Josh appears to have been ambivalent about being able to get help. If anything, his own experiences and his diagnosis did not 'match', and his behaviours worsened. Josh had indicators of disordered eating: his weight plummeted to nine stone. The clinicians who treated Josh identified anorexia, whereas he himself places more emphasis on his relationship with bingeing and purging, with his main experience at the time being that of securing affordable means to binge.

> I attended the clinic every Tuesday. At my worse I weighed around 9st and was told I exhibited behaviour of an anorexic. I had very little money and the food I ate didn't really matter. I didn't do normal shopping. Most money went on binge food and as I had very little it was often cheap crap, biscuits, sweets, things like that. Binging and purging took over my life. Bowls of oats and UHT milk with bags of sugar followed by laxatives were a common occurrence.

He spent most of what little money he had on bingeing. His preferred binge foods were broad in scope—what he binged on did not matter as long as he could binge. His foods were chosen by what was cheap, plentiful, and satiated the binge-need, rather than what was tasty. His purging was 'successful' in counteracting what food he did consume for a time, as mine was, leading to weight-loss despite being obsessed by eating as a response to every circumstance or emotional state. He had a tacit awareness that the food he force-fed himself with was of dreadful quality ('cheap crap'). He felt his shopping habits were not normal. It seems that he only did binge-shopping by this point and was no longer feigning doing a 'normal' weekly or monthly shop.

These binge-purges became his entire existence. The urge to binge and purge becomes a sole response to any daily living problem, as well as the automatic method of coping with larger pain that is being pushed aside or down. He binged on high-starch bulky food in the form of oats, with long-life UHT milk. It is perhaps not surprising he also used bags of sugar to flavour and sweeten the bowls of dry stodge; given the blandness of the oats on their own. What oats lack in taste, they make up for in terms of sheer bulk and inexpensiveness. This feels like a milder version of something I have experienced, called food concocting (Boggiano et al. 2013), although his mixture was not as 'bizarre' as my own. Food concocting involves taking a wide-ranging mixture of foods and eating them in bulk in combination. This is as opposed to preparing a meal whereby common food groups, whether deemed healthy or unhealthy, are arranged together without unnecessarily being mixed. It can involve mixing combinations of foodstuffs that others may find bizarre or unpalatable and any subtlety of flavour is eclipsed by a single facet: 'sweet' or 'salty', depending upon preference. Ultimately, Josh's concoction is not unusual in its most ordinary sense (cereals with milk and sprinkled with sugar) but the amounts and precise ingredient choice remind me of this.

Bingers choose food by immediate availability, and often select carbohydrates of varying types (Tanofsky-Kraff et al. 2013). Sugar was also consumed in other forms such as bingeing on cheap biscuits and sweets. Sweet foodstuffs are popular among female bingers (Allison and Timmerman 2007), so Josh is not alone in these food choices, although there is an implication that his preferences do not 'match' reported gender preference. There is a question as to how far this is the experience of other men who binge: whether the foods are 'trigger' foods or simply a matter of circumstance and convenience—little to do with taste and far more to do with availability of quantity. Ralph Wilps (1990) bought bread and cheeses to binge on; whereas, Frank (Bruni 2009: 21) seemed to binge on more expensive foodstuffs such as takeaways amongst other things, although not exclusively so. As he says, "food that was only marginally appealing beat no food at all."

At some unspecified point, the man becomes aware that there is little else in his life other than bingeing and purging, and what little there is, is made to fit around the need to binge and purge. This can be framed as a realisation or 'awakening'. Josh shares a particular memory with clarity:

> I remember very clearly my first win over bulimia. I arrived at my flat with bags of food and pills and knew what would happen. As I began something kicked in, what the hell was I doing??? I grabbed every last bit of food and carried it to the bin store and threw it away, crying. I then went for a walk. I don't remember the walk, I must have covered miles. It was a horrid day.

His binge-purge was set, he had both his bags of food and his laxatives and was prepared for the binge event. He needed to go through with it and even went as far as to start but then there was a sudden questioning of his own automatic behaviour. What followed was an immensely powerful and courageous thing to do—to not only stop mid-binge but to see this through with an action to dispose of the food. This courage in breaking-off once having begun is enviable. Despite this bravery, his own actions caused him pain. After he had thrown the remaining food away, taking it outside to the bin store, rather than simply putting it in his kitchen bin (good idea—I would have ended up eating it later if it were just in the kitchen bin), he cried and ended up walking for miles clearly in a dissociative state.

Even though it was a 'win', the experience was not a happy one, the day is emblazoned on his mind as being horrible. Did he grieve the loss of the food? Did he regret that he had sabotaged his own 'relief', on which he had spent precious financial resource? Walking seems to feature a great deal for Josh, perhaps this is because it was cost-free and added to the feeling of purging—actively doing something to counteract the binge. In this instance, perhaps it was more how rhythmic and transporting it felt—with no real sense of time or distance he was able to lose himself.

Josh felt that this event marked a change in his bulimia, although he does not describe his way of gauging what he perceived as normal eating, he did feel as if things were improving and the grip of bingeing and purging was lessening.

> Over the next few years I got better, began to eat a little more normal, binges becoming less. [...] Since then I have often had the urge all over again. In actual fact, in hindsight, I think it would be fair to say I have binged since then. At work for example when food was left over from meetings. Piles of sandwiches, cakes, biscuits. At those times boy did I overindulge, in secret of course. No one has known until I write this. Definitely binge behaviour. My weight shot up; last year I weighed 16 stone. I started to diet with my wife a strict 1000 calorie a day diet. I now weigh 11 stone.

In exploring Josh's idea of becoming 'normal', Scott Simon (2006) also feels able to judge what people would normally consume, compared to the way he used to eat. Whereas, John Evans (2011) shares how his idea of normal is screwed-up and because of his anorexia he finds it difficult to judge. My own understanding of normal eating is constantly in flux, as I rediscover what it might be and what it means to others around me.

Josh's binge-purge life ended over ten years ago but he recognises that the urge remains. On occasion, this urge has been acted on but only the bingeing, not the purging response. A notable example being an excess of food in a workplace situation—a working lunch with food ordered in, free to employees. Both sweet and savoury snacks were finished off by him, as if nothing was allowed to be left or thrown away but only once everyone else had gone, of course. This resonates with my own experience, railing against a 'cavalier attitude' to wasting food by taking a personal responsibility for seeing that the food does not go to waste (Taylor et al. 2014).

A Different Fugly—Fat and Ugly

There's a sense that Josh has really committed a secret to paper in writing the story above as no-one knew that that is what had happened to the food at the work meeting—I am the first to read about it—and this does not feel surprising as it echoes intensely private, secret shames around behaviour perceived to be repulsive. For example, William Leith (2010) shares similar experiences of disgust at his own actions. As Josh stopped purging this meant a significant weight gain, which led to dislike of his new weight, so he began to diet. This is given a sense of legitimacy not only because it was not a binge-purge related secret restriction but also because it involved his partner, trying to lose weight together. This recollects Frank's (Bruni 2009) mother's collusion with him, dieting together and sharing diet books, tips and foodstuffs. Later, once away from home, Frank and his female best friend did highly-restrictive diets together, such as three-day 'cleanse' fasts where they only consumed water.

Given that women are more likely than men to engage in extreme weight-loss strategies (McCabe and Vincent 2003), perhaps Josh 'uses' the woman in his life to legitimise extreme dieting for weight-loss, as this can then be framed as 'not for him' but for his partner, to show support. This has a faint echo of Gough's (2018) observations about men's body project work, where diet and beauty are justified as being for the women in the men's lives. This is also born out in Gary Grahl's (2007) experiences with anorexia, which began life as a display of solidarity with his wife's attempts to slim.

His weight-loss from sixteen stone to eleven stone feels quite dramatic for only one year. Josh and his wife's diet allowed one thousand calories a day to achieve this and evokes an idea that this is a socially-sanctioned, sanitised version of his disordered eating still holding sway. His routine calorie restriction has settled at two thousand calories per day more recently and he admits to still finding it hard to eat beyond specific times of day. Josh thinks his issues with food are not something he sees as likely to come to a definitive end—not something that is 'curable', although he feels as if his bulimia has subsided.

> I still hate myself. I cannot stand the way I look. I think I am fat, I think I am ugly. I would like to write 'I know I am' rather than I think I am. [...] I think I will always have a problem. Not full on bulimia, that has now passed, I think. Yet it's not normal, surely, to dislike yourself so much as I do?

Despite losing the weight he was so disappointed to have put on, he continues to judge himself harshly for the way he looks. This goes further, deeper even, and is about how unattractive he feels he is—he cannot stand his looks, feeling he is fat and ugly. This calls to mind Ben, a male gym-goer: "I feel so out of control when I binge. I can't stop. I feel primitive, like an animal, like I never ate before. Then as soon as it's over, I feel guilty, repulsive, gluttonous, stupid, lazy, and fugly—that's my word for 'fucking ugly.'" (Pope et al. 2000: 136). Josh's version of 'fugly' is the simultaneous experiences of feeling fat and ugly.

This feels akin to a form of self-focused 'lookism' (Lyu and Gill 2012), where he is judging himself in a highly stigmatising and prejudicial way based purely on physical appearances. He is also aware that even this does not capture how strongly he feels, demonstrating impressive self-awareness; he wanted to phrase the statement about how he *feels* he is ugly as how he *knows* he is ugly. This frames his ugliness as a statement of fact, as something absolute that cannot be challenged by the reader, and therefore someone else cannot persuade him to think differently about himself. It is a painful note to end on that ultimately he acutely dislikes himself, whilst acknowledging that this self-hatred is not automatically the experience of other people—not a normal way to feel. He is not alone, however. Michael (Prager 2010) describes his intense bodily disgust and Simon Brooks (1997) shares Josh's fugly feelings.

Discussion

Developing Disordered Relationships with Food

Josh's story represents a previously unexplored aspect of disordered eating in males: the impact of a loved one's suicide on a man's own relationship with himself and food. This is of interest here because the development of an eating disorder tends to be presented as multi-factorial and multi-stage in both men and women, yet Josh foregrounds his brother's suicide as marking a single identifiable beginning of his mental health issues. Might this represent a challenge to what is currently known about the development of disordered eating?

Both the legacy of his brother's suicide and Josh's subsequent attempt to kill himself require further thought. Suicide has long been proven as being more prevalent in males in the West (Cleary 2012; Wyllie et al. 2012) and in eating disorders, this is known to be a significant aspect of the high mortality rates (Beat 2018). Durkheim (2002) frames three types of suicide: egoistic, altruistic and anomic suicide. The definitions that Durkheim offers are: emphasis on the individual with less importance placed on community integration within society can result in egoistic suicide; altruistic suicide involves a belief that the sacrifice of one's own life will lead to benefits for others or is necessary because the value of one's life is beyond physical existence; and disillusionment due disenfranchising social mores characterises anomic suicides. My meaning-making relies on the overlap between these. Whilst Josh's text does not detail what drove his brother to suicide, it is reasonable to assume that these types of internal struggle (lack of social bonds, feeling those around will be better off and disillusionment) may have factored into his brother's experiences.

Those bereaved by suicide can go on to experience "complicated grief" that can result in traumatic stress disorder (Chapple and Ziebland 2011: 173), which has been found to be connected to the development of disordered eating (Mitchell et al. 2012). This might support the idea that Josh's brother's death alone drove Josh to disordered eating. In addition, a generational, imitative nature to suicide has been posited. A man becomes accustomed to the idea (Durkheim 2002), following a lead already set. Just as a man might 'learn' suicide ideation (Mann 2002), might this not be the case for disordered eating? Josh's brother had issues with food and chose suicide, ergo, Josh followed in his footsteps. This would establish Josh's disordered eating as an imitative crisis management strategy. He continues and furthers his elder brother's issues with food, completing his "...destiny only in successive layers of generations." (Durkheim 2002: 289). As an aside, this could account for the prevalence of eating disorders within families more than biological findings about genetics.

Durkheim (2002: 2008) offers a final fascinating insight. In his proposition of the notion of anomic suicide, he creates an interesting linguistic connection between appetite, consumption and ending life:

> ...our capacity for feeling is in itself an insatiable and bottomless abyss... Unlimited desires are insatiable by definition and insatiability is rightly considered a sign of morbidity... Inextinguishable thirst is constantly renewed torture.

I am not suggesting that there is an intrinsic link between a compulsive desire for excessive food (bingeing) and the act of taking one's own life. Rather, this is notable here because of its framing: using a universal language of hunger and thirst to express the fulfilment and thwarting of emotional desire as being related to whether someone chooses to continue to live. And, in understanding Josh's text, the idea of 'being thwarted' is a significant one, as this is something that has not arisen in the qualitative literature about men so far.

Being thwarted when seeking belonging (rejection) and perceiving oneself as a burden to those around us are proposed as the two core elements that co-exist in those who commit suicide (Van Orden et al. 2010), along with social conditions of the disconnectedness in which this results (Wyllie et al. 2012). When this is part of a longer-term experience of feeling constantly assailed by, and therefore increasingly habituated to Cleary (2012), pain and fear (Van Orden et al. 2010) without being able to articulate precisely why and what effects this is having on him, a man can decide that not being alive is a viable option. The sheer number of painful and fear-inducing experiences given in Josh's text suggests that his suicide attempt was to be expected, given what he had endured.

To return to his brother's suicide. Whilst Josh's story emphasises the role the loss of his brother played and downplays the subsequent traumatic events he endured (merely cataloguing a plethora of emotional overwhelm), my interpretation of his text supports what we know from other eating disorder experiences: his brother's suicide as a single root-cause is too simplistic. Josh's disordered relationship with food owes more to the accumulation of: years of coping with early experiences of weight-related bullying; depression resulting from his brother's loss; rejection and feelings of worthlessness; maltreatment at the hands of others and the social isolation this caused, rather than being the result of a single, triggering crisis in the aftermath of his bereavement.

Challenging the Stoic Male

There are several aspects of this story that appear congruent with extant literature but others that challenge what assumptions we currently make when it comes to male behaviours around dieting, help-seeking, and receiving treatment. In empirical studies, there is often focus on treatment and recovery (for example Greenberg and Schoen 2008; Weltzin et al. 2012). The story interpreted in this chapter, however, depicts a significantly different focus. Treatment appears but detail is scant about his experiences of getting help. In addition, what can be seen is a dispassionately recorded contradiction between Josh's meaning-making and that of the medical establishment he was involved in, whereby he feels his life has revolved around bingeing and purging only to be diagnosed as anorexic. This example supports the evidence presented in Chap. 1 that diagnosis of men is problematic.

It is important to Josh to share his current behaviours with food, namely, he appears to have shared his strict dieting with his wife. The male diet is oft-represented as being unhealthy and detrimental to health in media portrayals. When newspapers do cover men dieting, instead of the culinary creations of male TV chefs, "…dieting is established as a female domain, an irrational place…" (Gough 2007: 335). When diet meals are extolled, these are presented in as manly a way as possible (liberal in words like 'substantial' or 'hearty'). Women should actively manage the diet of their 'tubby hubbies', leading on the nutrition that would prevent their men from lapsing into flabby, flaccid soft bodies (McPhail 2009). So, even when a society decides that men's nutrition is of concern, it is decidedly not for them to be preoccupied with, instead being the province of the women in their lives. Perhaps dieting specifically for weight-loss, as opposed to, for instance, muscle-building, is permissible as a dedicated pursuit when shared with a woman. In this way Josh's story exemplifies this female-male tandem in managing calorie consumption. This said, admitting to dieting at all would suggest that this story challenges some traditional stereotypes about women always dieting and men being supremely unconcerned.

There are other, complex ways in which Josh does not appear to follow what has been reported in the literature. Here I am referring to a common stereotype of men as "relationally challenged", being reluctant to articulate the need to pro-actively seek help (Addis and Mahalik 2003: 7). The story challenges a basic assumption of men not engaging well with mental health treatment (whereas, women are more likely to conceptualise unspecified distress as emotional issues and recognise that they would benefit from support). The layers of social implications are complicated. Asking for and accepting help involves myriad intrapersonal and interpersonal interactions: embracing reliance-on-others for well-being; being able to name and describe emotions and emotional states; relinquishing emotional control of internal experiences; and, finally, dealing with fear of adverse reactions by others towards the man who admits needing help. The latter is to adopt a different form of manhood, one that is dependent, contingent, and flawed. Despite this, Josh actively accessed treatment; he did not succumb to assumed notions of men as help-avoiders. In other words, he does not battle on entirely alone for his entire story. Although, he was clearly imbued with a need to be intrapersonally resilient, dealing with pain alone, silently keeping trauma and sensitive behaviours secret.

This can be conceptualised as being 'hardy'. That is to say, it is not that Josh should have no emotional life, indeed certain emotions are societally encouraged as being typically masculine, such as anger. Rather, hardiness is to be self-controlled, self-contained, and purposeful (Riska 2002). It could be argued that being hardy may well account for why Josh lists a number of life-altering, damaging events in such a plain inexpressive way, devoid of emotion. He has borne suicide and bodily violence. He was required to fend completely for himself, when he became homeless. He has kept the secret of his relapse bingeing until writing his account. Hardiness now seems too muted a term. Instead, stoic would be a more accurate description. In the simplest formulation, this is about the ingrained messages men internalise about not showing hurt (particularly emotional hurt), being able to keep control and being seen to be tough. This stoical aspect of manhood is further activated in response to shame. Suffering shame in silence and bearing secrets alone forms part of this self-reliance. As Kimmel (2008) suggests, silence is one of the ways we teach boys to be men, raising them to be "strong, silent, self-contained." (Lee and Owens 2002: 19). Yet, stoicism as a displayed response to adversity can lead to psychological issues, such as disordered eating (Botha 2012). At first glance, then, in Josh's story this stoicism certainly seems to be in evidence. Nonetheless, Josh did take the step of seeing a doctor and even went as far as accepting a referral to outpatient services. This challenges some of the more recent qualitative work that suggests men may refuse treatment, or drop-out, due to their experiences of being made to feel 'less than a man' (Räisänen and Hunt 2014).

However, what happened to Josh once he began receiving treatment causes us to return to recent findings in the literature that suggest that some men experience a disconnect between what healthcare professionals tell them and what they, themselves, are experiencing (Ahonen 2003; Räisänen and Hunt 2014). In Josh's case, the medical staff emphasised his weight-loss, whereas he was more concerned about his relationship with bingeing. They had declared him anorexic, yet his story contains an ebb and flow with both his habits and his weight fluctuating, and Josh clearly prioritising the effects of excess on his life. What this highlights is the extent of difference that can occur between interpretations. On one hand, there is the interpretative lens of the medical establishment, with an emphasis on diagnosis, using their accumulated nosological data to group people into treatable categories with predictable treatment pathways. On the other, is Josh, whose preoccupation is with counteracting bingeing through experiments in purging 'optimally'.

Fat and Ugly—The Fugly Man

Josh ended his account expressing his profound belief that he is fat and ugly. Here I add to Ben's meaning of fugly (fucking ugly), as Josh not only adds his dismay about his looks but his pain at being perceived as fat. Once again, this challenges even relatively recent research that men are disinterested, or even positive, about their looks. Mark Twain said "the worst loneliness is not to be comfortable with yourself" (cited in Corson and Andersen 2002: 198) but being comfortable in oneself is perhaps more and more elusive in a culture of "cosmetic gaze" (Lupton 2013: 70) that creates a societal imperative to constantly assess and reassess our bodies (Drummond 2005).

There is an important debt to be paid to feminism at this point. It has been the contention of feminist work that women's bodies have been the site of this objectifying gaze, with women under pressure to conform to men's ideals of feminine beauty. The works here are too numerous to mention but Bordo (2003), Orbach (2006) and Wolf (1990), along with texts whose basis is in eating disorders, such as those by Chernin (1981) and MacSween (1993) feature heavily in my thinking on the experiences shared by women, about women, on the heavy collective burden Western culture causes through its ideals of physical perfection.

As stated above, Josh's experiences have been contrary to men being typified as relatively immune to such expectations, instead adhering to other societal norms that have not traditionally been reliant upon an objectified beauty aesthetic (this is explored in more depth later in the book). For instance, where men were asked to evaluate their looks they were self-hopeful, perceiving the positive aspects when comparing themselves with others, as opposed to the self-critical perceptions when women were asked (Franzoi et al. 2011). It has also been suggested that men refrain from framing their own and other men's bodies in terms of physical beauty and appeal (Gough 2018; Grogan 2016), yet this is certainly not the case in Josh's experience of himself. These ideas are already succumbing to extensive re-exploration in this new century, and certainly, Josh would not agree with the quote that Gilmore (1994: 191) uses to discuss this very issue: "men are like bears, the uglier, the more handsome", as he finds his fugliness makes him loathsome.

Josh's experience of fugliness suggests that earlier assumptions that men are protected from being objectified are no longer the case. He appears to be subject to the powerful, internalised discourses that objectification brings. With this objectification comes the concept of 'lookism', the appearance-based discrimination against others has already been explored in feminism in relation to what women have to face on a daily basis (Katzman 1997). Being concerned about what others think of our appearance has been shown to factor into social cohesion in female groups (Lyu and Gill 2012). This is a useful way of viewing the changes that are said to be occurring within society for men: if discrimination on the grounds of physical appearance increase, then individual concern related to appearance is likely to increase. Despite this, the theory of lookism currently lacks an acknowledgement that men, too, are concerned about their appearance. In essence, it cannot take account of Josh's profoundly-experienced disdain for himself. In the past, male beauty was to be found less in a soft, voluptuous flesh and a symmetrical countenance and more in an ability to hold our own, able to draw on raw physical power: wielding, rather than yielding. Yet, male pre-occupation with the body as a lived, highly-visible depiction of our ability to self-regulate (Hesse-Biber 1996) is proliferating and Josh has not been immune to this.

Discussion of the body, as Josh has experienced his, therefore, is incomplete without brief consideration of fatness. Women who are overweight are un-beautiful, they are unworthy of being objects of either fantasised or actualised sexual desire, whereas men who become fat are weak-minded and lack self-control (McCabe and McGreevy 2011). It appears from Josh's text that already being publicly considered overweight preceded his preoccupations about being so. This implies that it was not fear of fatness that fuelled his early broken relationship with his body (and the food he put into it) but the response he received from others about his fatness. And this may be because what is being regulated is a person's right to embody being masculine. Soft, fat flesh is emasculating, dysfunctional (Monaghan 2007) and is a threat to masculinity (Gilmore 1994), not a positive expression of the care and abundance that patriarchal privilege affords: "...reviling fatness is not a peculiarly feminine preoccupation." (Bell and McNaughton 2007: 108). Josh is one example of the fact that men's bodies, their fatness, and the public responses to that fleshiness is no less complex, interwoven or socially-regulated than those of women (Gill et al. 2005). Given the complicated nature of being in possession of a fat male body, it is perhaps to be expected that this forms an integral distressing ending to Josh's text. It is clearly more important to males than is currently given credence. However, for further analysis of the concept of fat in relation to the male body, see Gareth's story and Chap. 6, as it requires further discussion once the other experiences have been explored.

References

Addis, M. E., & Mahalik, J. R. (2003). Men, Masculinity, and the Contexts of Help Seeking. *American Psychologist, 58*(1), 5–14.

Ahonen, P. S. (2003). *Men's Experience with Eating Disorders: Uncommon Lives? A Look at the Experiences of Men with Eating Disorders.* Chicago: Annual Conference of the American Educational Research Association.

Allison, S., & Timmerman, G. M. (2007). Anatomy of a Binge: Food Environment and Characteristics of Nonpurge Binge Episodes. *Eating Behaviors, 8*(1), 31–38.

Andersen, A. E. (Ed.). (1990). *Males with Eating Disorders.* New York: Brunner/Mazel.

Beat. (2018) *Eating Disorders Statistics.* Beat. Retrieved June 17, 2016, from https://www.b-eat.co.uk/about-beat/media-centre/information-and-statistics-about-eating-disorders.

Bell, K., & McNaughton, D. (2007). Feminism and the Invisible Fat Man. *Body & Society, 13*(1), 107–131.

Birmingham, C. L., Touyz, S., & Harbottle, J. (2009). Are Anorexia Nervosa and Bulimia Nervosa Separate Disorders? Challenging the 'Transdiagnostic' Theory of Eating Disorders. *European Eating Disorders Review, 17*(1), 2–13.

Boggiano, M. M., Turan, B., Maldonado, C. R., Oswald, K. D., & Shuman, E. S. (2013). Secretive Food Concocting in Binge Eating: Test of a Famine Hypothesis. *International Journal of Eating Disorders, 46*(3), 212–225.

Bordo, S. (2003). *Unbearable Weight: Feminism, Western Culture, and the Body.* Berkeley, CA: University of California Press.

Botha, D. (2012). *No Labels: Men in Relationship with Anorexia.* South Africa: Moonshine Media.

Brooks, S. (1997). Anorexia: A Male Perspective. In R. Shelley (Ed.), *Anorexics on Anorexia* (pp. 53–60). London: Jessica Kingsley Publishers.

Bruni, F. (2009). *Born Round: The Secret History of a Full-Time Eater.* New York: Penguin Press.

Bureau, J. S., Mageau, G. A., Vallerand, R. J., Rousseau, F. L., & Otis, J. (2012). Self-Determination: A Buffer against Suicide Ideation. *Suicide & Life-threatening Behavior, 42*(4), 377–393.

Campling, M. (2012). *The Nature of Anorexia and Recovery: A Heuristic Self-Search Inquiry*. (pp. 127). London: University of Wales.
Chan, T. W., Ahn, W. Y., Bates, J. E., Busemeyer, J. R., Guillaume, S., Redgrave, G. W., Danner, U. N., & Courtet, P. (2013). Differential Impairments Underlying Decision Making in Anorexia Nervosa and Bulimia Nervosa: A Cognitive Modeling Analysis. *International Journal of Eating Disorders, 47*(2), 157–167.
Chapple, A., & Ziebland, S. (2011). How the Internet Is Changing the Experience of Bereavement by Suicide: A Qualitative Study in the UK. *Health, 15*(2), 173–187.
Chernin, K. (1981). *Obsession, Reflections on the Tyranny of Slenderness*. New York: Harper & Row.
Cleary, A. (2012). Suicidal Action, Emotional Expression, and the Performance of Masculinities. *Social Science & Medicine, 74*(4), 498–505.
Cohn, L., & Lemberg, R. (Eds.). (2014). *Current Findings on Males with Eating Disorders*. Hove: Routledge.
Corson, P. W., & Andersen, A. E. (2002). Body Image Issues among Boys and Men. In T. F. Cash & T. Pruzinsky (Eds.), *Body Image: A Handbook of Theory, Research, and Clinical Practice* (pp. 192–199). New York: Guilford Press.
Culbert, K. M., Racine, S. E., & Klump, K. L. (2015). Research Review: What We Have Learned About the Causes of Eating Disorders—A Synthesis of Sociocultural, Psychological, and Biological Research. *Journal of Child Psychology and Psychiatry, 56*(11), 1141–1164.
Drummond, M. J. N. (2005). Men's Bodies: Listening to the Voices of Young Gay Men. *Men and Masculinities, 7*(3), 270–290.
Dubosc, A., Capitaine, M., Franko, D. L., Bui, E., Brunet, A., Chabrol, H., & Rodgers, R. F. (2012). Early Adult Sexual Assault and Disordered Eating: The Mediating Role of Posttraumatic Stress Symptoms. *Journal of Traumatic Stress, 25*(1), 50–56.
Durkheim, É. (2002). *Suicide*. Abingdon: Routledge Classics.
Evans, J. (2011). *Becoming John: Anorexia's Not Just for Girls*. Didcot: Xlibris.
Fairburn, C. G., & Harrison, P. J. (2003). Eating Disorders. *The Lancet, 361*(9355), 407–416.
Frank, A. W. (1995). *The Wounded Storyteller: Body, Illness, and Ethics*. Chicago: University of Chicago Press.
Frank, G. K., Roblek, T., Shott, M. E., Jappe, L. M., Rollin, M. D., Hagman, J. O., & Pryor, T. (2012). Heightened Fear of Uncertainty in Anorexia and Bulimia Nervosa. *International Journal of Eating Disorders, 45*(2), 227–232.
Franzoi, S. L., Vasquez, K., Sparapani, E., Frost, K., Martin, J., & Aebly, M. (2011). Exploring Body Comparison Tendencies: Women Are Self-Critical Whereas Men Are Self-Hopeful. *Psychology of Women Quarterly, 36*(1), 99–109.

Gill, R., Henwood, K., & McLean, C. (2005). Body Projects and the Regulation of Normative Masculinity. *Body & Society, 11*(1), 37–62.
Gilmore, D. D. (1994). The Beauty of the Beast: Male Body Imagery in Anthropological Perspective. In M. G. Winkler & L. B. Cole (Eds.), *The Good Body: Asceticism in Contemporary Culture* (pp. 191–214). Oxford: Berghahn Books.
Gough, B. (2007). 'Real Men Don't Diet': An Analysis of Contemporary Newspaper Representations of Men, Food and Health. *Social Science & Medicine, 64*(2), 326–337.
Gough, B. (2018). *Contemporary Masculinities: Embodiment, Emotion and Wellbeing*. Cham, Switzerland: Springer.
Grahl, G. A. (2007). *Skinny Boy: A Young Man's Battle and Triumph over Anorexia*. Clearfield, UT: American Legacy.
Greenberg, S. T., & Schoen, E. G. (2008). Males and Eating Disorders: Gender-Based Therapy for Eating Disorder Recovery. *Professional Psychology: Research and Practice, 39*(4), 464–471.
Grogan, S. (2016). *Body Image: Understanding Body Dissatisfaction in Men, Women and Children*. London: Routledge.
Gueguen, J., Godart, N., Chambry, J., Brun-Eberentz, A., Foulon, C., Divac Phd, S. M., Guelfi, J. D., Rouillon, F., Falissard, B., & Huas, C. (2012). Severe Anorexia Nervosa in Men: Comparison with Severe an in Women and Analysis of Mortality. *International Journal of Eating Disorders, 45*(4), 537–545.
Hesse-Biber, S. J. (1996). *Am I Thin Enough Yet?: The Cult of Thinness and the Commercialization of Identity*. Oxford: Oxford University Press.
Katzman, M. A. (1997). Getting the Difference Right: It's Power Not Gender That Matters. *European Eating Disorders Review, 5*(2), 71–74.
Kimmel, M. S. (2008). *Guyland: The Perilous World Where Boys Become Men*. London and New York: Harper.
Kingerlee, R. (2012). Conceptualizing Men: A Transdiagnostic Model of Male Distress. *Psychology and Psychotherapy, 85*(1), 83–99.
Lee, C., & Owens, R. G. (2002). *The Psychology of Men's Health*. London: Open University Press.
Leith, W. (2010). *The Hungry Years: Confessions of a Food Addict*. Anchor Canada.
Lupton, D. (2013). *Fat*. Abingdon: Routledge.
Lyu, M., & Gill, D. (2012). Perceived Physical Competence and Body Image as Predictors of Perceived Peer Acceptance in Adolescents. *Asian Journal of Social Psychology, 15*(1), 37–48.
MacSween, M. (1993). *Anorexic Bodies: A Feminist and Sociological Perspective on Anorexia Nervosa*. London: Routledge.
Madowitz, J., Knatz, S., Maginot, T., Crow, S., & Boutelle, K. (2012). Teasing, Depression and Unhealthy Weight Control Behaviour in Obese Children. *Pediatric Obesity, 7*(6), 446–452.

Mann, J. J. (2002). A Current Perspective of Suicide and Attempted Suicide. *Annals of Internal Medicine, 136*(4), 302–311.
McCabe, M. P., & McGreevy, S. J. (2011). Role of Media and Peers on Body Change Strategies among Adult Men: Is Body Size Important? *European Eating Disorders Review, 19*(5), 438–446.
McCabe, M. P., & Vincent, M. A. (2003). The Role of Biodevelopmental and Psychological Factors in Disordered Eating among Adolescent Males and Females. *European Eating Disorders Review, 11*(4), 315–328.
McPhail, D. (2009). What to Do with the "Tubby Hubby?" "Obesity," the Crisis of Masculinity, and the Nuclear Family in Early Cold War Canada. *Antipode, 41*(5), 1021–1050.
Mitchell, J. E., Agras, S., Crow, S., Halmi, K., Fairburn, C. G., Bryson, S., & Kraemer, H. (2011). Stepped Care and Cognitive-Behavioural Therapy for Bulimia Nervosa: Randomised Trial. *British Journal of Psychiatry, 198*(5), 391–397.
Mitchell, K. S., Mazzeo, S. E., Schlesinger, M. R., Brewerton, T. D., & Smith, B. N. (2012). Comorbidity of Partial and Subthreshold PTSD among Men and Women with Eating Disorders in the National Comorbidity Survey-Replication Study. *International Journal of Eating Disorders, 45*(3), 307–315.
Monaghan, L. F. (2007). Body Mass Index, Masculinities and Moral Worth: Men's Critical Understandings of 'Appropriate' Weight-for-Height. *Sociology of Health & Illness, 29*(4), 584–609.
Nowakowski, M. E., McFarlane, T., & Cassin, S. (2013). Alexithymia and Eating Disorders: A Critical Review of the Literature. *Journal of Eating Disorders, 1*(21), 1–14.
Orbach, S. (2006). *Fat Is a Feminist Issue*. London: Arrow Books.
Pike, K. M., Wilfley, D., Hilbert, A., Fairburn, C. G., Dohm, F.-A., & Striegel-Moore, R. H. (2006). Antecedent Life Events of Binge-Eating Disorder. *Psychiatry Research, 142*(1), 19–29.
Pope, H., Phillips, K. A., & Olivardia, R. (2000). *The Adonis Complex: The Secret Crisis of Male Body Obsession*. New York: Simon and Schuster.
Prager, M. (2010). *Fat Boy Thin Man*. Los Gatos, CA: Smashwords.
Räisänen, U., & Hunt, K. (2014). The Role of Gendered Constructions of Eating Disorders in Delayed Help-Seeking in Men: A Qualitative Interview Study. *BMJ Open, 4*(4), 1–8.
Ridge, D., Emslie, C., & White, A. (2011). Understanding How Men Experience, Express and Cope with Mental Distress: Where Next? *Sociology of Health & Illness, 33*(1), 145–159.
Riska, E. (2002). From Type a Man to the Hardy Man: Masculinity and Health. *Sociology of Health & Illness, 24*(3), 347–358.
Russell, L., & Laszlo, B. (2013). A Group for Men with Eating Disorders: When "Lone Wolves" Come Together. *Men and Masculinities, 16*(2), 252–259.

Simon, S. (2006). *Male Bulimia: My Dark Demon.* Lincoln, NE: iUniverse.
Strother, E., Lemberg, R., Stanford, S. C., & Turberville, D. (2012). Eating Disorders in Men: Underdiagnosed, Undertreated, and Misunderstood. *Eating Behaviors, 20*(5), 346–355.
Strumia, R. (Ed.). (2011). *Eating Disorder in Males.* New York: Nova Science Publishers.
Tanofsky-Kraff, M., Bulik, C. M., Marcus, M. D., Striegel, R. H., Wilfley, D. E., Wonderlich, S. A., & Hudson, J. I. (2013). Binge Eating Disorder: The Next Generation of Research. *International Journal of Eating Disorders, 46*(3), 193–207.
Taylor, C., Webb, T. L., & Sheeran, P. (2014). 'I Deserve a Treat!': Justifications for Indulgence Undermine the Translation of Intentions into Action. *British Journal of Social Psychology, 53*(3), 501–520.
Van Orden, K. A., Witte, T. K., Cukrowicz, K. C., Braithwaite, S. R., Selby, E. A., & Joiner Jr., T. E. (2010). The Interpersonal Theory of Suicide. *Psychological Review, 117*(2), 575–600.
Weltzin, T. E., Cornella-Carlson, T., Fitzpatrick, M. E., Kennington, B., Bean, P., & Jefferies, C. (2012). Treatment Issues and Outcomes for Males with Eating Disorders. *Eating Disorders, 20*(5), 444–459.
White, A. A. H., Pratt, K. J., & Cottrill, C. (2018). The Relationship between Trauma and Weight Status among Adolescents in Eating Disorder Treatment. *Appetite, 129*, 62–69.
Williamson, I., & Hartley, P. (1998). British Research into the Increased Vulnerability of Young Gay Men to Eating Disturbance and Body Dissatisfaction. *European Eating Disorders Review, 6*(3), 160–170.
Wilps, R. F. (1990). Male Bulimia Nervosa: An Autobiographical Case Study. In A. E. Andersen (Ed.), *Males with Eating Disorders* (pp. 9–29). New York: Brunner/Mazel.
Witte, T. K., Didie, E. R., Menard, W., & Phillips, K. A. (2012). The Relationship between Body Dysmorphic Disorder Behaviors and the Acquired Capability for Suicide. *Suicide & Life-threatening Behavior, 42*(3), 318–331.
Wolf, N. (1990). *The Beauty Myth: How Images of Beauty Are Used against Women.* London: Random House.
Wyllie, C., Platt, S., Brownlie, J., Chandler, A., Connolly, S., Evans, R., Kennelly, B., Kirtley, O., Moore, G., O'Connor, R., & Scourfield, J. (2012). *Men, Suicide and Society: Why Disadvantaged Men in Mid-Life Die by Suicide.* Surrey: The Samaritans.

CHAPTER 3

Fat and the Wrecked Body

Abstract This chapter furthers ideas about men's experiences of fat and draws connections between body, identity and thwarted belonging, along with the effects of stigma and spoiled identity. Ambivalent experience of using online pro-eating disorders spaces is discussed. Prevalent findings about male ideals of muscularity are juxtaposed with a desire of slenderness. Sex, belonging, and desire in male eating disorders are explored.

Keywords Fat men • Sex • Stigma • Spoiled identity • Pro-Ana

The Story of Gareth

Gareth has tried to locate relevant information about male disordered eating and not been successful; as such, he sees the merit in further investigation into the topic. His weight was high from a young age, being twenty stones when only middle-teens. So, it is not merely a 'skewed perception' of an imagined weight, but a fact of his childhood. He was overweight in an obvious way and was acutely aware of it. This led to being bullied by both male and female pupils at school, which echoes the experiences found in other stories where men dealt with the humiliation of childhood overweight (McBride 2014; Ruiz 2008; Samuel 2008; Saxen 2007). Brian Cuban's (2013) story captures this well. He was terrified of having people see his 'gut' during 'shirts and skins' during school team sports. Shirts and skins was commonly used in all-male sports classes by Physical Education

R. Delderfield, *Male Eating Disorders*,
https://doi.org/10.1007/978-3-030-02535-9_3

teachers. Half the group would play a team sport with their gym attire complete ('shirts') and the other half would strip to the waist, shirtless ('skins'), to differentiate the opposing teams.

Escaping the Fat Boy

This abusiveness was far more than verbal. People treated him with disgust and contempt, even spitting at him.

> As a child, I was severely overweight. By the time I was 16–17, I weighed 20 stone. Beforehand, at school, I was seriously bullied kids boys and girls alike. Boys would spit, kick, punch and hurl vocal abuse, girls were somehow worse. The words they spoke could be vile, and a look could last forever. It was a horrible experience, school that is.

It was the reaction from girls that has stayed with him the most because of their saying mean, wounding things, and the way they looked at him. He conveys that it felt indiscriminate, coming from all sides, and all because of his weight and size. Their facial expressions, glances and cruel jibes felt harsher than physical bullying, though he did endure that too. Yet, currently it is suggested that it is girls who suffer more from this type of bullying (verbal and social), rather than boys (Farrow and Fox 2011; Smith and Gross 2006). By the time he finished school, his confidence and self-esteem was low: the damage had been done by this early point in his life (Copeland et al. 2015; Reece et al. 2015). At least a fresh start happened, because he transitioned to a sixth form college at the end of his compulsory education.

The fresh start also meant he had the chance to be a whole new person, redolent of a *Re-inventing Tara*-style story (Morrison 2002). Lennox Morrison's fictional tale is about complete personal reinvention, with an overweight, unattractive mistreated young woman emerging as a new person with a new appearance, physique and fresh personal values. It is a direct iteration of makeover culture, in which the new persona is everything she ever wanted to be, she feels sufficiently ashamed by her former self (and tries to conceal her old life) but she gets her true love in the end.

> I left school extremely lacking in confidence and went to a separate college that few if any kids I went to school attended. I wanted to loose weight to get a girlfriend, I thought that was how it worked, I also wanted to reinvent myself, having been given a new chance to start over.

This idea feels prevalent in today's society, full of makeovers, searching for potential in the 'ordinary people on the street', and reality television programmes. In the 'society of the spectacle' (Debord 1994), some intensive work, a makeover and a fresh start fixes everything. Gregg McBride's (2014) experiences appear to support this. His story is one of escaping his fat self and the culmination of this work is a 'before and after' television appearance, where he walks on to a camera-laden set in his new body, with hosts having just revealed photographs to the world of Gregg at his fattest (almost 33 stones). This feels as if this was what Gareth was hoping for following such a destructive school experience: he would lose weight and finally attract a girlfriend, as well as escaping his fugly past at his former school. As he became interested in girls, he equated weight-loss with attracting the opposite sex, making the automatic assumption that he would not attract someone, being overweight. A similar experience is shared by Brian (Cuban 2013), whose wish was to be thought of as a fit, attractive man above all else.

Wrecked—Ruined Life, Ruined Weight-Loss

Whilst he was still a teenager, his dad admitted that he had been cheating on his mum. Following this admission by his father, he began to feel low, anxiety set in, and this led to extremely rapid weight-loss.

> Not long after my 17th birthday, I found my father was having an affair, and fell into a state of depression. Throughout that year—while still trying to loose weight—I was very stressed and anxious. I lost 5 stone in a year, and continued to do so over the next year and a half.

Infidelity can become a catalyst for the onset of difficult personal problems for the children involved. In a perverse turn of events, Gareth got what he wanted (to shed weight) but not in its original, positive 'fresh start', self-recasting way. He turned his parents' relationship troubles in on himself and began a sustained period in which he diverted all of his negative emotions into losing weight, including purging and starving himself where necessary. This appears in other men's stories: where family factors beyond the man's immediate control are directed inwards, becoming a subject of introspection and personal blame. For example, Richard (Chap. 5) and Michael (Prager 2010) both report the effects that the break-up of their families had on them, and how it felt a like a starting point of the problems with food and self they then encountered.

Stress and disruption over three years resulted in his need for personal control gaining greater power over him, which he continued to centre on food and weight. His family circumstance was not the only thing to go awry. Gareth took a gap year before going on to university but, sadly, he experienced a further awful setback when he had an accident.

> Troubles from my 18th to 21st Birthdays continued and I took out all of the troubles out on my weight and eating habits (purging and fasting). I blamed myself for the divorce of my parents among many other things that were going wrong at the time.
>
> I took a year off before going to uni, and had an accident that left me immobile for a time, and as a result but on 2.5 stone. I was wrecked, so I worked hard on fasting and purging and by the end of my first year weighed 9.5 stone. I put on about a stone in the year since.

Experiencing significant life events like this have been linked to disordered eating (Mitchell et al. 2012) and in his case the accident resulted in a loss of control over his weight because it limited his mobility. This led to renewed weight gain, instead of the desired further weight-loss. He perceived this very negatively, not just as a setback but as a major problem that damaged him further. He describes himself as 'wrecked' at this point because a good deal of weight (two and a half stones) was gained over this time while his broken body healed. Being wrecked invokes the idea that he was beyond repair—a ruin of his former self—and that in addition to any psychological effects, there were physical ones deleterious to his body. Similarly, another man, Ron (Saxen 2007) described being 'damaged goods' because of being overweight. Wrecked, ruined or damaged, Gareth made a conscious effort to reduce his post-accident weight gain. For someone very heavy as an adolescent, dropping to nine and a half stones again (after having reached twenty stones) is a dramatic decrease in such a short time. Other men have shared how they have experienced radical weight-loss following periods of self-imposed non-eating. Michael Krasnow (1996), Ron (Saxen 2007), and Daniel (Samuel 2008) all lost significant amounts of weight rapidly. This takes significant determination to abstain from not just over-eating but regular eating on the part of these men. For Gareth, clearly, he was determined to salvage something from the wreckage.

At this time, his issues with depression came to the fore, set against the unknown newness of going to university for the first time. He interlinks the depression with patterns of disordered eating, both of which tend to interact with one-another rather than existing as separate mental health issues (Abebe et al. 2012; Striegel et al. 2012), and this interaction is known to be complex (Abbate-Daga et al. 2012).

> In the year since I was dragged down by depression and due to complications at university, had to leave at the beginning of this year. I now (at 22) live back at home and continue to take out my issues on my weight. Its become a way to vent for stress, depression and anxiety alike.

Unfortunately, Gareth then left university prematurely. Giving up on university cannot have been easy, letting go of independence and returning to live back at home. Ultimately, this feels like an overwhelming set of successive upheavals to have encountered in only twenty-two years. Yet, as with Josh, 'complications' at university, that could have been any number of disappointing or upsetting challenges, are stated in a matter-of-fact way, without further elaboration.

Gareth identifies that these continued changes were channelled into the way he felt about his weight, as a way to release stress, depression, and anxiety (Muehlenkamp et al. 2012) that are known to occur in men with disordered eating (Feltman and Ferraro 2011). This continues the idea of the 'punishing crucible' (Chap. 1), whereby the man's body is the site of a man's self-destructive ontological practices. In addition to his weight control being part of a stress coping mechanism, what is noticeable is that his behaviours over this period of his life were not about achieving a particularly masculine body ideal through muscularity, which is something that is often thought of as being what men want for their bodies (Keel and Forney 2013). Instead, he focused on being 'not fat'.

Skinny Girls Want Skinny Guys

Whilst some of his desire for thinness was related to being able to prove his persecutors wrong, proving that he could achieve a thin body, another aspect of his drive for slimness was about wanting to feel attractive, as mentioned above. Whilst Daniel (Samuel 2008) makes mention in his story of his disordered eating being linked to wanting to be attractive to the opposite sex, Gareth actually gauged his own attractiveness by those females to whom he felt attracted. Essentially, he would need to be skinny to attract thin women.

> I always wanted to be thin, even when I was the fat guy at school. In recent years, I've looked to pictures of women and the like I find attractive. I don't think that its that I want to be a skinny woman, rather that I think they would never like me or want to be with a guy like me, fat. I never wanted to be muscular and macho and large. I guess its because I was always big and strong anyway, being 20 stone gives you a lot of power. I wanted the opposite, to be worryingly thin.

This evokes ideas previously seen in, for example, *Attitude* magazine (a gay lifestyle magazine published online and in press by Attitude Media Ltd. in the UK) where a man described building a muscular physique deliberately to attract men he desired, who were, in turn, muscular and masculine-looking. This works on a premise of like-attracting-like. Gareth is adamant that girls he felt attracted to would never want to be with a fat man. In addition, there is an element of gender ambivalence in his own self-ideal—he had never hankered after a hyper-masculine form, as he felt he already had a version of this previously—the power and presence of a large man. Instead he needed the opposite to feel attractive: a dichotomous desire—an element of wanting something at exact odds with his predicated body build. Gareth disliked having over-size and strength. He did not want the assumed power that went with such a large frame, being as he was tall, as well as heavy. This desire for thinness has been found in other men (Grossbard et al. 2013; Herbozo et al. 2004) but what is striking here is Gareth's overt and unashamed affinity with something that is reported elsewhere as likely to cause gender role conflict because it does not conform with typified masculine ideals of how to outwardly present as a 'successful' man (Murray et al. 2013).

This different take on how to shape his body is something that Gareth emphasises; he wanted to be worryingly thin. This reveals that he already knew that the small size he wanted for himself was 'too far'.

> Maybe there's something in being so very petite and fragile, reminiscent of the benevolent youth I never really had; or the reverse in comments about my weight being too much to being too little, or simply that I genuinely have such a lack of faith in women, inasmuch as they are all shallow and judgemental like all the little girls were in school, and that all guys are egotistical bigheads that like to down tread the outsiders.

His description of what he wanted to be, petite and fragile, feels as if it would normally be attributed to a more feminine subject, yet Gareth is clear that he did not want to be a woman, just to attract women he admired. This goes beyond a desire for thinness and has a certain sense of gender ambiguity about it. His ideal is one more associated with 'femininity' in Western culture and sees Gareth revulsion at size and power transformed into attractiveness-through-vulnerability. His choice of words can also be associated with wanting to capture an aspect of childhood that he did not get to experience due to being overweight from such an early age. In this reading, what may be perceived as 'feminine' adjectives, instead capture a pre-pubescent boy's physique where the difference between size, form and build are non-existent between girls and boys, and physical genderedness is limited to genital difference (Ackard et al. 2001; Zehr et al. 2007). This has specific associations with my own story of ambivalence around masculinity, where my desperate desire to be smaller than I was feels like a response to being forced into an adult, maturing, male pubertal body before being ready to embrace such changes as a positive acquisition of manhood. I just wanted to take up a lot less space.

There does appear to be a damaged (toxic?) relationship with the opposite sex he wants to feel attraction from, something he refers to as 'a lack of faith'. He feels that adult women are as bad as the scathing cruelty and superficiality encountered from teenage girls at school, where they were never able to see beyond someone's size. Even during slimmer periods he has still felt judged by his weight or shape, and Gareth appears to not have female friends or companions who support and validate him just for being him.

A Daemon Needs Virtual Friends

As seen I the last extract, Gareth has also suffered for want of male friends: platonic intimates were let-downs, too—selfish and prone to thinking too much of themselves, judging their fellow males too quickly and harshly. Others reflect on their relationship with friends: James (next chapter) found that friends deserted him. John (Evans 2011) realised his only friends were his parents. Loneliness is signalled here, as he does not mention any friends who were able to offer him comfort, understanding, and a sense of belonging. To find this sense of belonging, Gareth's relationships have turned 'virtual'. When he cultivates online relationships, he is judged by his words and interactions, not his current physical shape and appearance.

> I've recently got onto a blogging website where people talk about their ED; ana, mia, and pro-ana groups. I genuinely so not condone pro-ana in anyone. I feel like a daemon on this site. They don't need to do this to themselves, but still I do it to myself, and we all say the same thing to each other. It does encourage our ED, but at the same time, there is consoling and a level of support that keeps it in check.

This has the potential to be worrying, however, as he is achieving this through engagement in pro-Ana or pro-Mia chatrooms and websites. He makes a powerful statement when he says that he feels like a daemon on the websites. It has shades of devious, manipulative or destructive actions. This archaic spelling of a word, usually used to evoke the image of an evil spirit, can also mean someone skilful and adept at their craft—a meaning which seems to fit with mastery of pro-Ana behaviours. It calls to mind "…men have long encountered 'the devil in their flesh'." (Bell and McNaughton 2007: 108), where the man's body constitutes and is constituted by the wickedness of a lack of control, of the immorality of fat and the unwholesome actions of a man given over to out-of-control lusts.

Gareth shares that there is a level of consolation and feeling of being supported on the websites, as does Jim Kohl (2009)—the only other man who reports interacting with pro-Ana spaces in his story—even though it ultimately feeds the disordered eating and despite the fact he does not condone what happens in pro-Ana and pro-Mia spaces. I can see that finding friends in a pro-Ana space is better than having no community or friendship at all. Nonetheless, I find this particularly challenging. It subverts my experience of support formats that are designed to instil hope of a sustainable recovery, free of the eating disorder, rather than promote maintenance of self-destructive behaviours and habits.

> I don't have any intentions of stopping my lifestyle in the foreseeable future.

It makes for an uncomfortable understanding of Gareth's experience: recovery, in the typical sense (learning to overcome and manage the mental health condition), does not feature in Gareth's immediate future. Not only is he matter-of-fact about his weight-related self-harming behaviours but he is chillingly pro-status quo.

Discussion

Fat Men Ain't 'Sexy'—Fat and the Wrecked Body

Gareth was a large boy as a teenager, so his relationship with a fleshy form of his self was created early on in his life; as such he had a certain experience of his body that was already prevalent before he became an adult. His body is "...simultaneously material and representational" (Robertson 2006: 451), our bodies share a message with the world around us. The space we exist in bodily is not just physical but becomes part of our interaction with the culture in which we live. Bodies can convey meanings beyond their physicality, they can represent how we feel about ourselves, how we feel about others and can be a source of positivity and nurturance or negativity and shame (Orbach 2009), or they can present an internal ambiguity about the way masculinities or femininities are embodied. The corporeal and conceptual experience emerging from this text is one of 'fat'. As a young fat man, Gareth encountered painful rejection and systematic abuse due to his weight.

Whilst he is not alone in this, as demonstrated by the other stories that are referenced in my interpretation, Gareth's experiences do raise the issue of what it means to be fat for men who develop disordered eating. Some of the behaviours he was exposed to were more akin to the way people would treat undesirables on the street. People lashed out at him and spat at him, expressing unbidden disgust and contempt for the person he was. Gareth was treated as if he were something inherently wrong, evil, even. This malevolence against the fat man is on the increase (Bell and McNaughton 2007). Men are not immune to being demonised for their appearance, and they are all too aware of the real flesh of their imperfect bodies (Robertson 2006). Within this, fat is stigmatised as dysfunctional and defective (Gilman 2004). Indeed, the links between fatness and illness are already well established "...in a shame and blame culture where fatness is authoritatively equated with emasculating sickness..." (Monaghan 2007: 605).

In Gareth's text, to be fat means to be weak-willed (McCabe and McGreevy 2011); to be diminished and derided; to be subjected to public displays of disapproval and hatred, cruelly persecuted and spoken to maliciously, with words having an irrepressible power to force Gareth to confront the devil in his flesh; and that he is wrong to the core. Moreover, to be fat is to have a spoiled identity (Goffman 1963; Temple Newhook et al.

2015), tainted and stigmatised before anyone has chance to know the person beneath the flesh. Gareth's body begins to undergo change to this outward appearance, something he hopes will allow people to evaluate him differently, only to be involved in a debilitating accident that sees his fat creep back and ruin his re-invention. By this time he is wrecked, his body is broken, it is big, unwieldy and malfunctioning. Not only is he damaged but he succumbs once again to the diabolical wickedness of fat flesh.

Worse, perhaps, depending on point of view, is that to be fat is to be sexless, undesired and overlooked, something which affected Gareth deeply and which accords with Gilman's (2004) work on the societal implications of fat male bodies where overweight men are metaphorically neutered. Gareth wanted a romantic partner, this was a driving force in his desire to reinvent himself, but as Frank Bruni (2009) notes, fat made him a sexual Switzerland: entirely neutral in matters of sex, not so detached from sex that others could not talk to him about their own sex lives but so devoid of sex that no one ever assumed him to even have an interest in conducting sexual intercourse with someone.

However, there is another framing of size within male discourse, which is one of robustness and power, to be oversized and strong, impervious to attack (Temple Newhook et al. 2015), a discourse that is available to men but not acceptably available to women. Yet Gareth challenges this.

Challenging the Muscular Ideal—"Indisputable Slimness" (Bruni 2009: 154)

In history, if there was a previous link between being dominant and large through affluence and corpulence as marks of wealth and power (Gilman 2004), this has been predominantly displaced by a current prevalence for 'hard' bodies (Alexander 2003) in the West, with the male body becoming a project as much as the female body (Gill et al. 2005; Gough 2018). The male body is now a commodity to be styled and honed through physical and aesthetic attention (Bordo 1999; Luciano 2002; Simpson 2013), with the demands on men's physique being dislocated from the reality of men's lives: as men's bodies are subject to less and less physical jobs through the economic necessity of our society, their bodies are expected to reflect a by-gone era of physical labour. In essence, many men (though by no means all) are in sedentary lifestyles of desk-jobs and cerebral exertions (the brain of a banker), the images pressed upon them for their body is that of a Herculean, sculpted physique (the body of a warrior).

Indeed, in order to be sexually appealing, the male body has been theorised as becoming increasingly muscular (Heath et al. 2016), with some men going to extreme lengths to achieve this goal (Murray et al. 2016). To have a hard body is to be the opposite of the fleshy, sinfully-slothful, corpulent man. Where unshapely, yielding flesh is soft; sculpted, unyielding muscle is hard. Men are choosing muscle because it is *not* fat (Peterson and Anderson 2012), it is the antithesis of fat and cannot be mistaken for fat. Take the example of a male chest. Both a highly muscular male and a highly overweight male may have greatly developed protrusions in the chest area. But in the overweight man these are mockingly termed man-boobs or 'moobs' (Gough 2018) and perceived as male-flesh-turned-feminine, and therefore bad; whereas in the highly muscular male these are perceived as well-defined pectorals, whose rippling, swollen double-breastedness are a badge of honour and seen to be the epitome of masculinity, where the male body is *the* symbol of being virile, powerful and unquestionably masculine (Filiault 2010; Gattario et al. 2015).

Into this binary of hard- versus soft-bodied enters Gareth's text. His desire not for muscle but for slenderness contradicts this alleged societal trend towards muscular men. He does not pursue muscle; he does, however, want to be thin. This pursuit of thinness, in itself, is not unheard of in men (Murray and Touyz 2012). Rather, it is the reason driving his pursuit of thinness that has yet to be found in the literature: Gareth wants a body that is slender, like the women he feels attracted to. This is an important addition to an understanding of disordered eating. Gareth is not only driven to be slim as an antidote to his fatness per se, he wants to be found attractive and this is conflated with matching his body type with those he finds attractive. He will not succeed in attracting female attention unless he is able to mirror their slenderness. For Gareth 'skinny girls want skinny guys'. Gareth is questing for a slenderness and beauty that he did not feel he had the opportunity to enjoy in his youth, this, he feels, will save him from a life mired in cruelty and pain and provide him with the chance for much-valued belonging and closeness.

There is an added dimension to this however, as introduced in the section above. While Gareth does point out that he does not wish to be a woman, it is notable that some of the adjectives he uses to describe his preferred physicality are indisputably normally associated with feminine bodies and demeanors: 'petite' and 'fragile'. This represents a disavowal of the transgenderedness, for which we all have a capacity. For him he wanted a 'smallness' and fragility, a youthful boy-ish body, one that he had been robbed the chance of experiencing because of his teenage weight. What may be perceived as 'feminine' adjectives, instead capture a pre-pubescent boy's physique where the difference between size, form and build are non-existent between girls and boys. However, there is also the issue of desire. Gareth did not desire to be the powerhouse of a man he could have drawn on as a large man. Rejecting fat, therefore, is more than a pursuit of thinness. It is an attempt to feel safe instead of exposed (Pinto-Gouveia et al. 2012), ordinary instead of behemoth, whilst enjoying an adolescent-esque frame, one in which lost time can be made up for and Gareth is allowed to feel justified (and affirmed) in having sexual desires and affections for women to whom he feels attracted.

Embracing Pro-Ana

Gareth's embrace of pro-Ana is unique within the stories I have gathered, yet as seen in Chap. 1, there is evidence that men are using these online spaces. There are two aspects which require further discussion here. Firstly, there is a conflicted identity at work, as he uses the space to support his own slimming behaviours whilst feeling that he does not approve the nature of the online space he is using. Secondly, Gareth's engagement with pro-Ana marks the first time in the interpretative work where I struggle with fusing text and interpreter socio-cultural context, which bears further scrutiny.

Pro-Ana spaces largely involve chatrooms and discussion boards where those seeking to maintain rather than disconnect from their anorexia (or bulimia) can find friendship and support (Juarez et al. 2012). The disordered eating is given a name, 'Ana' (or 'Mia' in the case of bulimia) and are then often spoken (written) of as if they were identities in their own right (Brotsky and Giles 2007). This is not unheard of for males with eating disorders to so name and process their disordered eating in this way. For example, Joe (Langley 2006), in which Joe's mother writes the story of her son's anorexia from a family perspective, named his anorexia 'Rex'. This helped Joe dissociate from the totality of the disorder that was holding him captive, controlling and killing him. It also gave his family a name they could use to talk to Joe about his illness that felt detached from a clinical description of mental ill-health behaviours, whilst acknowledging the power of the hold that Rex had over everyone at home.

Gareth's identity work, as seen in his text, is one of reinvention from fat man to slender man (see above) and involves embracing a thin ideal as being desirous above all else (Day and Keys 2008). This thin ideal is one at odds with itself, as usually within pro-Ana spaces it has been found that users present their self-imposed starvation as being due to a naturally low appetite, where pursuing thinness is side-lined as a reason for starving. Instead users (predominantly female) follow discourses of fighting to be allowed to be as thin as they 'naturally are' in a world obsessed with making them eat more. In Gareth's text, however, there is an open admission to wanting the slender ideal, there is even an 'acceptable' reason—he wants to find mutual sexual attraction with the opposite sex. Gareth does not hide his agenda. As a former fat person, he is all too aware that being slim is part of his body project to re-make himself and that his use of the site is helping him to achieve this, as well as simultaneously bridging the loneliness and isolation he feels because he can make friends without being judged by appearance.

In the pro-Ana discourse, Ana is also constructed as a voice of resistance. Ana fights for people's rights to be the thinnest they can be without succumbing to medical intervention (Day and Keys 2008). It is about resisting a medicalisation as 'ill', whilst reframing the self-in-relationship with anorexia as a healthy lifestyle choice that can be managed successfully with the right tools and support. However, I would suggest that Gareth is not resisting a medical discourse around underweight and starvation so much as resisting a return to his former fat self. His battle is not with the medical establishment, indeed, he appears to have had very little contact with them other than his accident. Instead, he is using pro-Ana to maintain a reinvented version of himself where he can be cast as thin, whilst having the slim version of himself validated at the same time as meeting women he may find attractive.

My research engagement with this topic shows that the act of interpretation is revelatory. It highlights how researchers are not immune to becoming indoctrinated with certain messages. My use of language and the assumptions that this reveals merit brief consideration. Gareth is clearly coping as he sees best, making use of pro-Ana spaces to do this. Yet, I found myself railing against this because of a belief that pro-Ana spaces are inherently destructive and do more to prolong the disordered eating rather than inspiring recovery and freedom from the behaviours and thoughts. I-as-researcher had to overcome an automatically-experienced personal prejudice in order to remain as close to Gareth's text as possible.

My language in the interpretation suggests that at the point of immersion in the text, I was still framing Gareth's experience negatively, see the word 'chillingly' for example, where I portray his maintenance behaviours as something that are cause for concern. Gareth clearly does not share this view; however, terming himself a 'daemon' does suggest that he recognises his own destructive behaviour. Pro-Ana is where he has been able to build an identity outside of the confines of physical appearance, he is able to pursue his behaviours without fear of judgement or reprisal and may even gain tips in how to do this whilst maintaining some degree of healthfulness, as well as finding like-minded friends. Furthermore, Gareth's behaviours seem to be at odds with what Campling would describe as the 'colonisation' of the person by the eating disorder (Campling 2012; Williams et al. 2015). Can a man be colonised by his eating disorder if he, in fact, welcomes it and preserves it as a meaningful status quo? Gareth may not condone pro-Ana sites but he clearly draws from them to get through his life as it is, without feeling the need to change this at present. Finally, this maintenance of his disordered eating, with no intent to stop, marks a difference from many of the other male stories I have gathered, as there is no clear 'recovery message' shared with the reader. The behaviours are in stasis, we are left to accept where Gareth is, and the story despite drawing to a close, does not end there.

References

Abbate-Daga, G., Marzola, E., Gramaglia, C., Brustolin, A., Campisi, S., De-Bacco, C., Amianto, F., & Fassino, S. (2012). Emotions in Eating Disorders: Changes of Anger Control after an Emotion-Focused Day Hospital Treatment. *European Eating Disorders Review, 20*(6), 496–501.

Abebe, D. S., Lien, L., & von Soest, T. (2012). The Development of Bulimic Symptoms from Adolescence to Young Adulthood in Females and Males: A Population-Based Longitudinal Cohort Study. *International Journal of Eating Disorders, 45*(6), 737–745.

Ackard, D. M., Neumark-Sztainer, D., Hannan, P. J., French, S., & Story, M. (2001). Binge and Purge Behavior among Adolescents: Associations with Sexual and Physical Abuse in a Nationally Representative Sample: The Commonwealth Fund Survey. *Child Abuse and Neglect, 25*(6), 771–785.

Alexander, S. M. (2003). Stylish Hard Bodies: Branded Masculinity in Men's Health Magazine. *Sociological Perspectives, 46*(4), 535–554.

Bell, K., & McNaughton, D. (2007). Feminism and the Invisible Fat Man. *Body & Society, 13*(1), 107–131.

Bordo, S. (1999). *The Male Body*. New York: Farrar, Straus and Giroux.
Brotsky, S. R., & Giles, D. (2007). Inside the "Pro-Ana" Community: A Covert Online Participant Observation. *Eating Disorders, 15*(2), 93–109.
Bruni, F. (2009). *Born Round: The Secret History of a Full-Time Eater*. New York: Penguin Press.
Campling, M. (2012). *The Nature of Anorexia and Recovery: A Heuristic Self-Search Inquiry*. (pp. 127). London: University of Wales.
Copeland, W. E., Bulik, C. M., Zucker, N., Wolke, D., Lereya, S. T., & Costello, E. J. (2015). Does Childhood Bullying Predict Eating Disorder Symptoms? A Prospective, Longitudinal Analysis. *International Journal of Eating Disorders, 48*(8), 1141–1149.
Cuban, B. (2013). *Shattered Image: My Triumph over Body Dysmorphic Disorder*. Canyon Country, CA: NetMinds.
Day, K., & Keys, T. (2008). Starving in Cyberspace: A Discourse Analysis of Pro-Eating-Disorder Websites. *Journal of Gender Studies, 17*(1), 1–15.
Debord, G. (1994). *The Society of the Spectacle*. New York: Zone Books.
Evans, J. (2011). *Becoming John: Anorexia's Not Just for Girls*. Didcot: Xlibris.
Farrow, C. V., & Fox, C. L. (2011). Gender Differences in the Relationships between Bullying at School and Unhealthy Eating and Shape-Related Attitudes and Behaviours. *British Journal of Educational Psychology, 81*(3), 409–420.
Feltman, K. A., & Ferraro, F. R. (2011). Preliminary Data on Risk Factors and Disordered Eating in Male College Students. *Current Psychology, 30*(2), 194–202.
Filiault, S. M. (2010). *Gay and Lesbian Issues and Psychology Review*. Australia: Gay & Lesbian Issues & Psychology Interest Group of the Australian Psychological Society.
Gattario, K. H., Frisén, A., Fuller-Tyszkiewicz, M., Ricciardelli, L. A., Diedrichs, P. C., Yager, Z., Franko, D. L., & Smolak, L. (2015). How Is Men's Conformity to Masculine Norms Related to Their Body Image? Masculinity and Muscularity across Western Countries. *Psychology of Men & Masculinity, 16*(3), 337–347.
Gill, R., Henwood, K., & McLean, C. (2005). Body Projects and the Regulation of Normative Masculinity. *Body & Society, 11*(1), 37–62.
Gilman, S. L. (2004). *Fat Boys: A Slim Book*. Lincoln, NE: University of Nebraska Press.
Goffman, E. (1963). *Stigma: Notes on the Management of Spoiled Identity*. London: Simon and Schuster.
Gough, B. (2018). *Contemporary Masculinities: Embodiment, Emotion and Wellbeing*. Cham, Switzerland: Springer.
Grossbard, J. R., Atkins, D. C., Geisner, I. M., & Larimer, M. E. (2013). Does Depressed Mood Moderate the Influence of Drive for Thinness and Muscularity on Eating Disorder Symptoms among College Men? *Psychology of Men & Masculinity, 14*(3), 281–287.

Heath, B., Tod, D. A., Kannis-Dymand, L., & Lovell, G. P. (2016). The Relationship between Objectification Theory and Muscle Dysmorphia Characteristics in Men. *Psychology of Men & Masculinity, 17*(3), 297–308.

Herbozo, S., Tantleff-Dunn, S., Gokee-Larose, J., & Thompson, J. K. (2004). Beauty and Thinness Messages in Children's Media: A Content Analysis. *Eating Disorders, 12*(1), 21–34.

Juarez, L., Soto, E., & Pritchard, M. E. (2012). Drive for Muscularity and Drive for Thinness: The Impact of Pro-Anorexia Websites. *Eating Disorders, 20*(2), 99–112.

Keel, P. K., & Forney, K. J. (2013). Psychosocial Risk Factors for Eating Disorders. *International Journal of Eating Disorders, 46*(5), 433–439.

Kohl, J. (2009). *Skeletal Marriage*. San Jose, CA: CreateSpace.

Krasnow, M. (1996). *My Life as a Male Anorexic*. New York: Harrington Park Press.

Langley, J. (2006). *Boys Get Anorexia Too: Coping with Male Eating Disorders in the Family*. London: SAGE Publications.

Luciano, L. (2002). *Looking Good: Male Body Image in Modern America*. London: Macmillan.

McBride, G. (2014). *Weightless: My Life as a Fat Man and How I Escaped*. New York: Central Recovery Press, LLC.

McCabe, M. P., & McGreevy, S. J. (2011). Role of Media and Peers on Body Change Strategies among Adult Men: Is Body Size Important? *European Eating Disorders Review, 19*(5), 438–446.

Mitchell, K. S., Mazzeo, S. E., Schlesinger, M. R., Brewerton, T. D., & Smith, B. N. (2012). Comorbidity of Partial and Subthreshold PTSD among Men and Women with Eating Disorders in the National Comorbidity Survey-Replication Study. *International Journal of Eating Disorders, 45*(3), 307–315.

Monaghan, L. F. (2007). Body Mass Index, Masculinities and Moral Worth: Men's Critical Understandings of 'Appropriate' Weight-for-Height. *Sociology of Health & Illness, 29*(4), 584–609.

Morrison, L. (2002). *Re-Inventing Tara*. London: Sphere.

Muehlenkamp, J. J., Peat, C. M., Claes, L., & Smits, D. (2012). Self-Injury and Disordered Eating: Expressing Emotion Dysregulation through the Body. *Suicide & Life-threatening Behavior, 42*(4), 416–425.

Murray, S. B., Griffiths, S., & Mond, J. M. (2016). Evolving Eating Disorder Psychopathology: Conceptualising Muscularity-Oriented Disordered Eating. *The British Journal of Psychiatry, 208*(5), 414–415.

Murray, S. B., Rieger, E., Karlov, L., & Touyz, S. W. (2013). Masculinity and Femininity in the Divergence of Male Body Image Concerns. *International Journal of Eating Disorders, 1*(11), 1–8.

Murray, S. B., & Touyz, S. W. (2012). Masculinity, Femininity and Male Body Image: A Recipe for Future Research. *International Journal of Men's Health, 11*(3), 227–239.

Orbach, S. (2009). *Bodies.* London: Macmillan.
Peterson, G. T., & Anderson, E. (2012). The Performance of Softer Masculinities on the University Dance Floor. *The Journal of Men's Studies, 20*(1), 3–15.
Pinto-Gouveia, J., Ferreira, C., & Duarte, C. (2012). Thinness in the Pursuit for Social Safeness: An Integrative Model of Social Rank Mentality to Explain Eating Psychopathology. *Clinical Psychology & Psychotherapy, 21*(2), 154–165.
Prager, M. (2010). *Fat Boy Thin Man.* Los Gatos, CA: Smashwords.
Reece, L. J., Bissell, P., & Copeland, R. J. (2015). 'I Just Don't Want to Get Bullied Anymore, Then I Can Lead a Normal Life'; Insights into Life as an Obese Adolescent and Their Views on Obesity Treatment. *Health Expectations, 19*(4), 897–907.
Robertson, S. (2006). "I've Been Like a Coiled Spring This Last Week": Embodied Masculinity and Health. *Sociology of Health & Illness, 28*(4), 433–456.
Ruiz, R. (2008). The Ghost of Gordolfo Gelatino. In K. Taylor (Ed.), *Going Hungry: Writers on Desire, Self-Denial, and Overcoming Anorexia* (pp. 149–166). New York: Anchor Books.
Samuel, D. G. (2008). The Tale of an Anorexic Male Medical Student. *British Medical Journal, 336*(7649), 892–892.
Saxen, R. (2007). *The Good Eater: The True Story of One Man's Struggle with Binge Eating Disorder.* Oakland, CA: New Harbinger.
Simpson, M. (2013). *Metrosexy: A 21st Century Self-Love Story.* CreateSpace Independent Publishing Platform.
Smith, R. G., & Gross, A. M. (2006). Bullying: Prevalence and the Effect of Age and Gender. *Child & Family Behavior Therapy, 28*(4), 13–37.
Striegel, R. H., Bedrosian, R., Wang, C., & Schwartz, S. (2012). Why Men Should Be Included in Research on Binge Eating: Results from a Comparison of Psychosocial Impairment in Men and Women. *International Journal of Eating Disorders, 45*(2), 233–240.
Temple Newhook, J., Gregory, D., & Twells, L. (2015). 'Fat Girls' and 'Big Guys': Gendered Meanings of Weight Loss Surgery. *Sociology of Health & Illness, 37*(5), 653–667.
Williams, K., King, J., & Fox, J. R. (2015). Sense of Self and Anorexia Nervosa: A Grounded Theory. *Psychology and Psychotherapy: Theory, Research and Practice, 88*(1), 1–18.
Zehr, J. L., Culbert, K. M., Sisk, C. L., & Klump, K. L. (2007). An Association of Early Puberty with Disordered Eating and Anxiety in a Population of Undergraduate Women and Men. *Hormones and Behavior, 52*(4), 427–435.

CHAPTER 4

Punishment and Passing

Abstract Male anorexia is analysed with compulsive exercise as a key element. Parallels are drawn between food and exercise, and crime and punishment as concepts to understand the man's tortured relationship with restriction. Relationships with mum, friends and girlfriends on the man's eating disorder are discussed, including perfectionism and social withdrawal. Recovery is debated, especially stigma's impact on healthcare-avoidance. This is related to the idea of passing as 'normal' in eating disorders.

Keywords Excessive exercise • Stigma • Spoiled identity • Passing • Punishment

The Story of James

James was in the midst of an environment of disordered eating in terms of his friendship group, many of his friends struggled with their own eating issues, so he had prior experience of people trying to recover. This is the first man's story where I have come across this: that the person already knew many others with disordered eating.

> Unfortunately eating disorders surround me, as a number of my friends have either been bulimic or anorexic and one is currently trying to recover from anorexia. That friend is the one who made me realise I also had a problem, although I refused to accept it… In fact I was angry at her for a while for even suggesting it…

R. Delderfield, *Male Eating Disorders*,
https://doi.org/10.1007/978-3-030-02535-9_4

His use of the word 'surround' makes me wonder whether he felt penned in. An anorexic female friend first pointed out that James too had food issues but he was resistant to this observation at first. This resistance took the form of actually being cross with his friend for broaching it with him; he felt accused of being eating disordered. This was in spite of her being right. This is echoed in Jim's (Kohl 2009) negative reactions to his work colleagues, who challenged him about his low weight. By the time James did accept what his friend had observed, he realised that his problem had existed for five years.

Earning the Right to Eat

Originally, James felt the beginning of his behaviours to be unremarkable and innocent. He enjoyed exercise (swimming, for preference), he did so much that he lost weight and this invoked positive feelings even though it was fitness, not weight-loss itself, that motivated his exercising. The idea of enjoyment does not quite capture the buzz that can then become a must-have for those men who become addicted to exercise (Norris et al. 2012), myself included.

Unfortunately, a cycle began, one that was made more dangerous as there was no meal plan to compensate for additional calories burnt through exercise. Instead, he changed his food intake, not to nutritionally balance his diet and exercise, but to omit all foods considered unhealthy. These were not judged by 'health' but by what he perceived to be bad foods, where banned foods were based on erroneous, misleading and constantly changing public health information about healthy eating (Boylan et al. 2012).

> My problem revolves around compulsive exercise and many of the traits of anorexia. [...] It all started innocently enough by me trying to get a bit fitter while I was in university by swimming a few times a week (which I enjoyed). I started losing weight, quite liked that feeling, so continued to increase the exercise without really increasing what I ate (if I exercised I would have three meals a day) and changed my eating habits to something I felt was more healthy, cutting out anything I considered unhealthy and punishing myself if I ate any of these foods.

There then began a system of self-sanctions if he lapsed and consumed the foods that had been forbidden. This is enormously punitive and became *not* about the satisfaction of losing weight (James had never been heavy anyway to begin with) (Chan et al. 2013) but of challenging 'bad' eating decisions with a consequence. The punishing element is a thread that can be found in Jim's (Kohl 2009) story too, where he had to earn the right to eat.

> In terms of my weight for many years technically I didn't lose that much weight (although I've always been quite thin), however because I was still developing and growing when it started I should have been putting on weight naturally as I grew- that never happened.

This came at a time when he forestalled his body's natural development when his body was continuing to grow and develop in late puberty (Zehr et al. 2007). This is something that is thought to be common within young girls with anorexia (Bruch 1973), where natural development is disturbed by malnutrition, so it is interesting to see James's observation of something similar without any further commentary about what it means for growing into his male body.

He took every opportunity to be active while at university: he walked everywhere he could, cycled where he could not, played team sports and swam without considering a food intake adjustment, such as adding appropriate carbohydrates.

> …it got to the stage where I would run or swim every morning for about half an hour. If I swam I would also cycle to the pool, a round trip of four miles (not flat). In addition to this while I was in university I would walk everywhere, cycle to campus and play football a couple of times a week without eating any more. Exercise would be done seven days a week, regardless of the weather and regardless of any injury or illness.

The habit became a set routine of cardiovascular exercise but this also included his actual journey to and from the pool. What others would struggle to find the willpower to do, James engaged in as a matter of course, meaning he did not factor a long and gruelling round trip into his exercise regime. There is a sense of nostalgia that I guiltily feel when reading his exercise regime, as I fondly remember something I once held dear. My own addiction to exercise facilitated a constant distraction from the way I felt about my body (which I hated, see Chap. 1) and allowed relief from the effects and pain of bingeing.

James's compulsion was thrown into even starker relief when he had to incorporate working at a paid job it led to some unorthodox and extreme decisions of when to fit in exercising, such as getting up at 3 a.m. to go running before a long shift.

> ...now in the world of work, I have on occasions got up at 3 a.m. to go for a run because I knew I would be working a long shift but HAD to exercise. Not only that but my work was very active, and once again I cycled to and from work with the return journey including a long and steep climb. There were times I've been for a run in agony due to an injury, but ignored it because I HAD to exercise to be able to eat.

This exercise was augmented by both the physical demands of his work and the exertion of the daily commute by bicycle. There were not even any rest days; it was relentless and unforgiving, regardless of his circumstances. When injury or illness did occur they were barely taken into account (Morgan 2008). To others this must seem a rather pitiless way to treat the body, lacking any sort of self-soothing care.

James identifies similarities between his behaviours and those of a friend with Obsessive Compulsive Disorder (OCD), which positions this excess as necessary, as it wards off unwanted bad feelings and low self-image.

> ...at my worst, I had to exercise a particular amount every day and eat very similar things, if I didn't then something bad would happen! We also have very similar anxieties around relationships ... believing we are capable of controlling every aspect of a relationship and over analysing every conversation we have with other people, so as to ensure we haven't upset anybody or that what we have said can't be interpreted in a negative way.

Whilst these obsessive-compulsive behaviours have been linked to eating disorders in the female literature (Anderluh et al. 2003), this is something that other men have not done so far. James's likening of his behaviours to OCD highlights the role of a fear, of being scared of that which is difficult to control: other people and their unknown responses. Once this fear becomes overwhelming, it can no longer be reasoned with, and adhering to his compulsive and obsessive food restriction and exercise behaviours feels like the only way to establish control. This highlights a form of ontological insecurity (Laing 1960) where maladaptive strategies can take hold as we defend against threats to our self. For instance, he pays minute attention to everything said, to second-guess whether someone may have perceived him negatively and aimed to redress, remediate or reduce the likelihood of this wherever possible. James sees his need for control as being about suppressing many things—negative thoughts about himself, an inability to heal hurts or ward off potential harm and bury unwelcome emotional responses.

Even when his body was screaming for help he continued to be physically active without taking on more calories. The equation was simple: to win the right to eat at all, enough exercise had to happen—it was a brutal trade-off. This is something which is also found in Thomas Holbrook's (2000) story: *you can only have X, if you merit it from doing Y.*

> There were other occasions where I was so tired I was barely capable of running any further due to no energy and feeling faint. If I went away for the weekend and ate something I thought I shouldn't or knew that I would be unable to exercise that day I would cut out a meal, or reduce my portion size, simply because I thought I had to punish myself for eating something unhealthy or for not exercising. Not punishing myself would leave me agitated and anxious.

This extended into tit-for-tat compensatory behaviour if weekends were occupied in a way that did not allow for exercise: he had not earned the right to food, so he reduced his intake (for James this took the form of cutting entire meals or drastically reducing portions). This established a credit and debit system relationship between food and exercise, one that represents an extreme of a cultural norm in Western society where points awarded or forfeited, or 'sins' are accrued based on engagement with a weight-loss programme (examples of such programmes would be Weight Watchers™ and Slimming World™).

However, this went beyond a mere balancing act—he had to be punished or there would be a negative emotional pay-off through feeling anxious and agitated (O'Dea and Abraham 2002), so this becomes less 'credit and debit' and more 'crime and punishment'. The two words (anxious and agitated) do not quite convey the unbearable level of emotional pressure that would build if he were unable to punish himself. Despite a very bad time in final year at university, due to his obsessive exercising and food restriction, James went on to graduate. With hindsight he recognises that there was not only food and exercise issues but what must have been a severe depression, as it included suicide ideation with constant feelings of self-worthlessness and shame at who he felt he was; an immensely painful place to be in, although he makes no connection between his depression and his disordered eating. The shame and depression resulted in deliberate withdrawal from social life without a real awareness of what this would do to his friends (Watson and Nesdale 2012).

Withdrawing from Friends

Some friends walked away, others were terribly upset, as there was no obvious reason for James turning his back on them. When he did see people, he chose methods of socialising that meant as little investment of himself as possible, such as going to see films (less time for social interaction), or even more damaging to his own behaviours and sense of self—hanging out with people he cared little for or did not really know. This felt like less of a risk—if he did not know them they would be unlikely to have an opinion (or even be inquisitive) about his behaviours and habits.

> I had thoughts of suicide for a period and felt worthless throughout, ashamed to be who I was. Therefore I withdrew from all of my friends, and tried to keep myself to myself. This meant I lost some friends and hurt others because they couldn't understand what I was doing. If I did socialise I tried to go to the cinema around the corner because then I wouldn't have to talk to the people I went with. Alternatively I would socialise with people I didn't really know or didn't particularly want to socialise with!

Despite the darkness of the suicide ideation, he remained functional, however, which included getting and keeping a job but the social withdrawal continued and people were held at a distance—work was not exploited as a new opportunity to make friends. Exercise had to be top priority and socialising and relaxing were firmly in second place, which also meant he had to down-play and lie about the importance of exercise, to spare himself from being judged by others who objected to being second to his fitness regime.

Intimate relationships with the opposite sex were not really given any chance to blossom as he pre-empted the girl deciding that he was not worth bothering about (Paterson 2004). Other stories have also managed to capture the difficulty of being able to be open, honest and vulnerable within a relationship when the stakes feel too high and self-protection kicks in Cuban (2013) and Evans (2011).

> As for girlfriends I wouldn't give them long enough for them to get to know me because in my mind I knew I was worthless and that they'd soon find that out! So as soon as I felt they were getting to know too much about me, I would completely withdraw with no explanation, I also tended to be with people I wasn't too bothered about because it then didn't matter too much when the relationship inevitably ended.

Choosing to be with people he was not fulfilled by was a strategy he used to actively manage the emotional fall-out when a relationship ended, and he never doubted that relationships would end. This has a hollow quality to it: if he did not care about a person then he would not care if she walked away. This immunity and dispassion is something I can appreciate, I even entered a series of nonsensical relationships when my disordered eating was at its worst, seeing people I was not remotely interested in because then it would not hurt if it fell apart. Ultimately, not caring fulfils many functions, amongst which: it protects from having to attend to what others think and feel; it confirms one's worthlessness and keeps this from being challenged by meaningful attachments; and it maintains safety within a status quo of isolation.

As soon as he stopped denying or fighting the disorder that had taken over him, he wanted to understand how and why this had come to be, and his conclusion about this is unequivocal: he believes it to be because of his childhood and the way he was brought up.

> Since accepting it I have been determined to understand why I'm like this and unfortunately I believe a lot if it comes down to my upbringing. As a child I moved house a number of times, something I found very difficult as I am quite shy and can find it difficult to make friends. Therefore by the time I felt comfortable with people it seemed we would always move.

There was a considerable amount of upheaval because of moving to a new home multiple times and these moves affected a shy child, who already had trouble forming new connections. Finding maladaptive ways to compensate for being shy is something that is a developmental factor in many cases where a man experiences mental health issues (Watson and Nesdale 2012). With James, just as he was beginning to find his feet he had been moved on, subjected to the stress of having to make friends and be the 'new arrival' all over again, creating a fragile sense of self-worth.

Parents and Perfectionism

Having to make new friends repeatedly went hand-in-hand with a mum who did not give him the time or focus he needed and he is clear that any emotional expression was not permitted (Corstorphine 2006). He is not alone in this: other men (Evans 2011; Kohl 2009) have experienced a similar injunction on feelings, I certainly have. If emotional displays are embargoed then they are often turned inward instead.

> ...my mother [never...] showed any interest in me and emotions were a definite no-no. As a child I knew no better, saw my friends' mothers showing affection to them and therefore firmly believed the lack of affection from my mum was my fault. My answer was to try harder in school [...] just to be praised by my mum. Unfortunately this never came and hence my belief I was a disappointment and worthless. If my mother was ashamed of me, then why would anyone else give a damn about me? This all created a perfectionist side of me, where no matter what I had to be the perfect son, friend, boyfriend, student, worker etc.

He did not realise at first but as he grew up, he was exposed to different types of mothering via friends where there was warmth unconditionally given. The only difference, therefore, was him—so he attributed his mum's lack of warmth and responsiveness to himself—it was his fault. What James does not mention at any point is his dad, or any other significant male parent-figure. He simply does not factor in or he has been deliberately omitted from James's story.

As a result, he sought other ways to gain his mother's attention and regard, if not through an affectionate relationship, then through less intimacy-reliant methods. He tried to do well at school but this still did not really attract her notice, praise or approval. Ultimately, nothing brought this, so a natural conclusion was that he really did not matter. This led to a larger, less-rational leap in his mind, which was that if James brought shame on his own mother then there was no way he would attract the notice, praise and approval of anyone else. He had to be better because he just was not trying hard enough—the lack of validation proved that—so he had to be perfect in every way in all of his relationships. This perfectionist driver is known to feature in anorexia-related disorders (Cohn and Lemberg 2014). However, this is a grim and unforgiving place to be in psychologically as it is not attainable.

A negative response to praise became an automatic response for James—he discounted any validation of him as deception or not really intended by the giver. He disregarded anything that challenged his fixed perception of himself as worthless. A feeling of connection was still wanted, however, so he achieved this successfully by making other people the focus of the conversation—he became their confidante, letting them talk all about themselves but then this meant he had to be a secret-keeper for others in addition to all those secrets of his own, with which he was already dealing. Needless to say, this resonated strongly with some of my own experiences of these behaviours that reinforce an internal message that the listener is of little worth, while the person who is talking matters more.

James perceives his other key relationship, with food and exercise, as being a mechanism for control over such destructively negative feelings about himself.

> Eating and exercise initially became a way of controlling how I felt about myself (the only thing in my life I felt I could control), making me believe I was a little better than I thought, although this soon lost its impact and took control of me.

In a sense it worked, as it helped him to feel in control, that life was bearable and that it was all manageable and 'better' but it soon became *he* who was gripped by *it* instead. He hit a realisation that he was not going to be able to move forward but he also felt resistant to interfering with his eating and exercise behaviours because work was still going OK: if it was not broken why fix it? Or, more likely, this resistance emanated from a fear that life would completely fall apart without his behaviours (a form of identity disruption, Bury 1982). Various things transpired to help James realise how gripped by the disorder he had become. On holiday, as he could not guarantee his exercise quota, he controlled what he could—namely, his food intake. No calories and nutrients, however, meant a lack of energy and health to enjoy what should have been a memorable holiday. Instead, his trip was spent feeling poorly, lightheaded and unable to participate—something that feels distinctly sad and is evidence of just how much issues with food can impair someone's life.

Accepting that his carefully scheduled plans, behaviours and self-dialogue were damaging led to some clearer and more nurturing thinking for James. The next big step in his process was sharing this with a friend and it seems that this definitive action was needed to begin changing.

> Although of course this was the scariest part because you are admitting to yourself what you're doing isn't right and that you have to change the habits and routines you thought were all OK, the rational side of me was finally fighting back. Accepting to my friend I had a problem was the start of what has been a very difficult and often frustrating … recovery process, however I would now say I am back in control. My rational voice generally overpowers the irrational voice.

James judges the back-in-control element (despite how twisted things had been) as being able to tell the difference between rational and irrational self-dialogue. This raises the issue of what is rational versus irrational. Here, James appears to equate the irrational with something uncontrollable and suppressed within his upbringing: emotion. Whereas, rationality is associated with control. This is a common concept within Western thought (Seidler 1989) and is problematic here as James has already displayed significant issues with what he perceives to be control through his damaging relationship with diet and physical activity.

Recovery Without the Stigma

James decided he would work on recovering without any professional help. This reads like a brave decision but he felt clear about what it was that drove him to forego professional or clinical support: negative associations, the stigma that goes with an eating disorder.

> I am attempting to recover without any formal professional help (so far successfully). This decision not to get professional help was down to the stigma involved with having an eating disorder. In my previous job I had to notify work about any mental health conditions and yet in reality the work side of my life has been manageable its my personal life that was a mess.

This stigma has already been indicated as a significant factor in what we know about disordered eating men (Griffiths et al. 2014; Knightsmith et al. 2013) and suggests recovering by himself was borne out of fear. A practical example clearly explains his thinking: he had been employed previously in a workplace that expected to be notified of any mental health issues and this did not make sense to him, as it would feel like messing up something that so far was a positive element of his life—his work. This link with work is something that needs further investigation, as in my own situation I only knew how desperately I needed help once it had started to impact on my work. The lack of clarity of public understanding of disordered eating (and other mental health issues, for that matter) does not instil confidence when disclosing to employers or work colleagues. The perceived or actual stigmatisation and level of mistaken assumptions make sharing information about disordered eating too much to contemplate (Austen and Griffiths 2018; Griffiths, Mond et al. 2015; Griffiths, Mitchison et al. 2018; Zwickert and Rieger 2013).

Indeed, for James the greatest impact of his disordered eating was on his non-work life. He gained much from accepting that he had disordered eating as this opened the door to arming himself with information about how he had come to have eating issues. He had considerable resources to draw on, given the number of experiencers he already knew as friends. So, he tapped into an 'inherited' body of understanding from people around him, rather than health professionals.

> This takes time however and at first I probably tried to do too much too soon, probably a typical perfectionist! [...] My approach however has been to be completely open with my closest friends, this means they can then spot anything untoward, so I don't get away with lying to them. [...] I also recognise that the perfectionist side of me can be a good thing and that it is OK to make mistakes and be upset occasionally.

This feels like an unusual take on this because James sought to understand disordered eating from the people who know them best from a first-hand perspective, rather than through clinical interactions. However, this also evidences a persistent distrust of the medical establishment in favour of lay information. At the beginning of his recovery process he rushed and there is an understanding that the process is far from smooth and linear. He has adopted total openness with friends so that they can help him. This openness has been two-way—he was receptive to some of the good, warm messages they could give him about who he is and what he adds to their lives, and he has tried to stop automatically discounting them, instead he used them to widen his self-perception and reframe his perfectionism as something that has its uses but that should not be a blanket state of being. James no longer sees disordered eating as his identity, it is just a coping method that got out of control.

Discussion

Crime and Punishment

Over time exercise becomes bound up with emotional states (Batchelor 2012). Consistent with findings about compulsive and excessive exercising (Young et al. 2018), James would fit in time to exercise even if this meant going to extreme lengths, such as working out at unorthodox hours of the day, and he would continue to exercise even when injury would have required rest and recuperation. What is different here, and something that has as yet gone unrecorded in men, is the relational nature between eating and exercise. James had an interlocking connection between the two. There are two facets to this. Firstly, he had to earn the right to eat by completing the necessary amount of exercise. If the 'right' amount, within the boundaries decided by James, was not undertaken then this led to the withholding of foods as a compensatory activity that would see him foregoing meals. Secondly, if he indulged in eating foods that he perceived to be 'bad', then this would result in the need for sanctions to be imposed and would involve additional exercise to redress this, even in the face of exhaustion or injury.

In the interpretation I refer to this, at first, as a credit and debit system where every withdrawal resulted in a necessary compensatory deposit but this does not seem to fully capture the nature of what was taking place. It seems too abstract and removed from the experience that James was living with. The crucial missing element is one of 'pain'. Pain is what leads to this being an issue of crime and punishment, and pain is experienced bodily. Once again, then, I look to the body. If it is accepted that our emotional lives are not set apart from the body, then any discussion of the relationship between James, exercise and food becomes necessarily a bodily one. The body is the locus (the crucible?) of this interaction of crime and punishment. After all, "thought *is* bodily action" (Burkitt 1999: 79, original emphasis) and it has been suggested that men, in particular, perceive their bodies as instruments of action, of 'doing' (Seidler 1997).

There is more than one meaning of pain (Orbach 2009), and this is certainly the case when exploring disordered eating. James experienced the rush of self-control that his denial gave him: he denied his real physical pain from excessive exercising, he denied himself 'bad' foods in order to ostensibly achieve good health whilst in reality following an ever-decreasing regimen of acceptable foods and amounts to consume. In his self-denial and endurance of pain lay the tangible experience of control. In compulsive exercise, pain can be seen as an "anti-language" (Williams and Bendelow 1998: 2010). It dissolves the self-enabling capacities of the experiencer, focusing him on nothing but sensation. Pain is framed as both inevitable and desirable as it permits James's body to feel without having to concentrate on anything outside of himself and his immediate moment. In this way, pain is both a system of punishment for whenever an infraction is committed and a reward that evidences progress and affords an illusion of commitment and sacrifice.

So far, this suggests that James's body is an instrumental, physical and emotional monad (Burkitt 2008): an individual item, in touch with its own experience but divorced from a wider world. However, I would argue that this is far from the case. Our identity is not constructed based on an inner experience devoid of socialisation, rather it is formed within and informed by the culture we inhabit (Eakin 1999). This being the case, what does this mean for James's experience? It suggests that James, far from being a tabula rasa that the disordered eating can occupy, has come to relate to the world he occupies via his dialogue of crime and punishment. Our culture is awash with public health messages about fitness, the avoidance of obesity and indolence-related diseases (Boylan et al. 2012). There are ideas of what is healthy to do and to consume constantly on display as we grow up. James did not suddenly decide to place precedence on exercising and food abstinence above all else of his own accord, as if he was influenced innately. These are constructs that are to be found in the society in which he has developed his coping mechanism.

We are impelled to take care of ourselves to avoid becoming a burden on others or on the state, more than this, we are placed in a position of sanctioning against the body's desires whether this be for love, status or food (Bordo 2003). Our bodies are to be mastered and subdued to keep them acceptable (Chernin 1981). This is what James's system achieves: it subverts emotional struggles into a seemingly manageable two-way relationship of right-versus wrong. This means the body in James's disordered eating is the lived space for a self-regulated social morality (Chernin 1981).

Fractured Relationships

If the disordered eating body itself is deeply interwoven with the society and culture in which it is lived out, it makes sense that our interpersonal relationships are intrinsic to the way we come to relate to ourselves as men with disordered eating. In my interpretation of James's story three core aspects of relationships come to the fore: his relationship with his mother, his relationship with the opposite sex, and his relationships with friends.

In many texts about masculinities and about disordered eating, a psychoanalytic lens is utilised to understand the dynamics of parent and child (Moss 2012; Orbach 2005). However, here I will use a relational perspective to briefly analyse the impact of James's mother on his disordered eating. To do so I draw on ideas from Burkitt's (2008) work about the social nature of selves and how our sense of identity develops in response to the people we experience around us. Above I argued that as individuals we do not exist as isolated selves in a vacuum beyond the reach and influence of others around us. Rather, as beings we are constructed through the relations we have with others, and we are "populated by their voices" (Burkitt 2012: 471).

This has important implications, ones that James himself realises, when it comes to relationships with parents, carers and other guardians. James's mother appears to have been cold and distant towards her son. Despite trying to win her approval through means that were available to him she did not provide him with the recognition that he so desperately wanted. This lack of recognition calls into question our own sense of reality, as substantiation of our self-as-real is dependent upon others. James turned inward to make sense of this lack of response. He ascertained that he was lacking in some way.

This sets his relationship with his mother as something beyond his control and yet he so much wanted to influence her affection for him. James will have been operating from a place that is societally informed: mothers are supposed to love their sons. Yet something did not work within his home. His introspective response to the lack of recognition from his mother was compounded by a crucial exchange with our culture; he witnessed other sons' relationships with their mothers among his friends. This crystallised a realisation that the determining factor in this case was James himself. He alone was responsible for his mother's indifference, he was not worthy enough to merit attention and praise (Orbach 2009). As our feelings about ourselves are influenced by the way others respond to us (Burkitt 2012), this is not an illogical decision to make on his part. What this suggests is that early on in James's childhood he had been placed in the position of looking to himself, rather than to others, for the reason why he was not treated the same as other people. This establishes the terrain that the disordered eating could later occupy, as it involved introspection and self-blame for why things went right or wrong.

This feeling of being unworthy of positive attention pervaded further experiences in his life, namely romantic attachments. James clearly did engage in relationships with girls, however, in the interpretation, I use the word 'hollow' to describe these. He would not allow the relationships to move beyond a certain point of emotional intimacy and this had the effect of pushing the other person away from him. This has the effect of keeping James isolated from others, reconfirming that he is 'right' and that he is not worthy of love and closeness, whilst protecting him from the potential vulnerability that intimacy might place him at risk of. This creates an idea of *in*-vulnerability, something that is not only evident in his romantic relationships but also in his relationship with himself, as shown above, for example, in his attitude to exercise, such as not taking breaks during bad weather or injury. Unbeknownst to James, this perpetuated the cycle established with his mother. He would withdraw from his girlfriends, which would make them feel unworthy and dismissed, and they in turn would separate from him. This dichotomy appears to characterise his entire story: he could not be the perfect boyfriend, yet being any sort of boyfriend is rendered impossible due to his withdrawal from his romantic partner.

The subject of 'withdrawal' becomes an important one when exploring James's relationships with friends. James used self-fulfilling strategies when it came to these relations. He fostered 'plastic' relationships (Steiner and Perry 1997), whereby the people he was friends with did not really matter to him and did not actually know him. This allowed him to maintain distance and remain disengaged from those he was spending time with, thus reducing their threat to his vulnerable sense of self. He even put effort into working out that certain social pursuits were less personally intensive than others, permitting a facsimile of socialisation whilst keeping himself closed off. His worthlessness meant that he would discount any positive interaction with friends, so even if he did experience real connection that resulted in positive feedback about who he was, he was able to convince himself that these connections were unintended, mediated by alcohol or simply lies from people trying to make him feel better. His exercise regime contributed to this social withdrawal, as it he would maintain distance from others so as to not have to explain that any friends would only be secondary to his need for exercise.

What, then, is the result of such a scarce set of social connections and intimates? I would suggest that: "...selves that have emerged from extremely fractured social relationships can become divided by the contradictory messages that others communicate to them." (Burkitt and Sullivan 2009: 574). The positive messages from his friends seemed alien in light of the messages from his mother and the separations he endured as part of romantic relationships. How could he be a good, worthy person when his experience had taught him otherwise? Over time, his broken social relationships simply compounded his worthlessness and fuelled his retreat into compulsive exercise with disordered eating, as he lived in a form of social oblivion (Pirani and Varga 2005). This can be considered as the colonising action of the disordered eating (Campling 2012). This notion frames the disordered eating as a relationship, one that comes to occupy prime space for the man concerned. He no longer needs to work at relationships with anyone else. His main relationship is with his regimen of moralising about food and maintaining an exercise regime in order to be the perfect version of himself that no-one can love because no-one can get close, no matter how close to perfection he comes. These routines of exercise above-all-else, and extreme focus on food intake, form a response to "the dread of dissolution into non-being" (Laing 1960: 77). I return to this idea in Chap. 6, when ontological (in)security, which emerges in the interpretation above, is discussed in greater detail.

Passing as 'Normal'

People with disordered eating are known to have a strong "illness identity" and it has been suggested that this means that personal cure was not a possibility (Stockford et al. 2007: 148). James's experience would refute this clinical misconception. James has been working on his own recovery, using relationships around him with friends to check his self-development and remain true to himself, whilst paring back some of the ingrained habits that saw him desperate to feel well again.

Whilst his commitment to self-recovery alone is remarkable, what I want to focus on is the motivation behind his decision to recover without accessing health professionals. Despite the hardships discussed above, James did have one area of his life that he felt operated well: his work. This was a valued and necessary part of his everyday existence as his relationship with work is what compelled him to recover outside of health services. James shares that he did not want it to become known that he was eating disordered, as they monitored mental health needs. He wanted to safeguard that part of his life that he had protected from his disordered eating and where he experienced success, which meant not disclosing to work that he needed treatment. There is an argument here that James's refusal to seek professional help stems from a much-researched aspect of being a man, namely that asking for help is unmanly (Vogel et al. 2011) and that help-seeking is "anchored in femininities" (Oliffe et al. 2012: 512). In this way, it might be said that James evidences a somewhat typical male trait, that of 'going-it-alone' (the stoicism we discussed in Chap. 2), rather than admitting to others that help is needed.

However, this would be a mistaken interpretation. As James shares, he is more than willing to reach out to others for help, including his friendship group, especially as he knows others with disordered eating. What he is not prepared to do is to risk sacrificing his relationship with his workplace, he does not want them to have to know about what he has been dealing with due to his perception of becoming stigmatised. This leads us to a novel place because, whilst there is evidence in the literature about the stigma that men face when accessing health services (see Chap. 1), little is known about the nature of perceived stigma as it relates to men's recovery without clinical help. In James's case he "recognizes [his] stigmatized identity; [he] knows that [he] harbors a secret." (Young 2012: 2). It is the nature of this stigma that is so interesting in James's story. If we interpret stigma as being a social curse (Stevenson et al. 2014), a relational phenomenon that relies on our interconnectedness to others for it to affect us, then this makes it easy to understand why James would choose to recover without clinical support. After all, if our work offered us an unspoiled identity where we could feel success, who would willingly subject themselves to the "corrosive" (Stevenson et al. 2014: 2) and undermining effects of stigma, if there was the chance to avoid such a thing.

In this way, I would suggest that James had a real, felt sense of his spoiled identity (Goffman 1963) and wanted to preserve his sense of being non-disordered wherever he could. This is known as 'passing' (Frank 1995). In order for James to be able to preserve the work-life he valued, he had to be able to pass as a person who had no issues whatsoever. This has not been covered in the eating disorders literature thus far; however, it is discussed in depth in relation to other illnesses that are narrated by the sufferer (Frank 1995). James already felt worthless in other areas of his life, therefore he wanted to protect that which gave him genuine social value (Talley and Littlefield 2014), leaving it as unsullied and 'perfect' as possible. Revealing his flawed identity to healthcare services is to risk exposure (Goffman 1963), something which he was not prepared to do. Whilst Goffman would term James's passing as 'normal', phantom normalcy, it is clear that this is what has allowed James to avoid potential shame and pain. In turn, this has given him the personal space and freedom to seek recovery on his own terms, without fearing what others may say.

References

Anderluh, M. B., Tchanturia, K., Rabe-Hesketh, S., & Treasure, J. (2003). Childhood Obsessive-Compulsive Personality Traits in Adult Women with Eating Disorders: Defining a Broader Eating Disorder Phenotype. *American Journal of Psychiatry, 160*(2), 242–247.

Austen, E., & Griffiths, S. (2018). Why Do Men Stigmatize Individuals with Eating Disorders More Than Women? Experimental Evidence That Sex Differences in Conformity to Gender Norms, Not Biological Sex, Drive Eating Disorders' Stigmatization. *Eating Disorders*, 1–24. DOI: 10.1080/10640266.2018.1499337.

Batchelor, R. (2012). Thinking About the Gym: Greek Ideals, Newtonian Bodies and Exercise in Early Eighteenth-Century Britain. *Journal for Eighteenth-Century Studies, 35*(2), 185–197.

Bordo, S. (2003). *Unbearable Weight: Feminism, Western Culture, and the Body.* Berkeley, CA: University of California Press.

Boylan, S., Louie, J. C., & Gill, T. P. (2012). Consumer Response to Healthy Eating, Physical Activity and Weight-Related Recommendations: A Systematic Review. *Obesity Reviews, 13*(7), 606–617.

Bruch, H. (1973). *Eating Disorders: Obesity, Anorexia Nervosa, and the Person Within.* New York: Basic Books.

Burkitt, I. (1999). *Bodies of Thought: Embodiment, Identity and Modernity.* London: SAGE Publications.

Burkitt, I. (2008). *Social Selves: Theories of Self and Society.* London: SAGE Publications.

Burkitt, I. (2012). Emotional Reflexivity: Feeling, Emotion and Imagination in Reflexive Dialogues. *Sociology, 46*(3), 458–472.

Burkitt, I., & Sullivan, P. (2009). Embodied Ideas and Divided Selves: Revisiting Laing Via Bakhtin. *British Journal of Social Psychology, 48*(3), 563–577.

Bury, M. (1982). Chronic Illness as Biographical Disruption. *Sociology of Health & Illness, 4*(2), 167–182.

Campling, M. (2012). *The Nature of Anorexia and Recovery: A Heuristic Self-Search Inquiry.* (pp. 127). London: University of Wales.

Chan, T. W., Ahn, W. Y., Bates, J. E., Busemeyer, J. R., Guillaume, S., Redgrave, G. W., Danner, U. N., & Courtet, P. (2013). Differential Impairments Underlying Decision Making in Anorexia Nervosa and Bulimia Nervosa: A Cognitive Modeling Analysis. *International Journal of Eating Disorders, 47*(2), 157–167.

Chernin, K. (1981). *Obsession, Reflections on the Tyranny of Slenderness.* New York: Harper & Row.

Cohn, L., & Lemberg, R. (Eds.). (2014). *Current Findings on Males with Eating Disorders.* Hove: Routledge.

Corstorphine, E. (2006). Cognitive–Emotional–Behavioural Therapy for the Eating Disorders: Working with Beliefs About Emotions. *European Eating Disorders Review, 14*(6), 448–461.

Cuban, B. (2013). *Shattered Image: My Triumph over Body Dysmorphic Disorder.* Canyon Country, CA: NetMinds.

Eakin, P. J. (1999). *How Our Lives Become Stories: Making Selves.* New York: Cornell University Press.

Evans, J. (2011). *Becoming John: Anorexia's Not Just for Girls.* Didcot: Xlibris.

Frank, A. W. (1995). *The Wounded Storyteller: Body, Illness, and Ethics.* Chicago: University of Chicago Press.

Goffman, E. (1963). *Stigma: Notes on the Management of Spoiled Identity.* London: Simon and Schuster.

Griffiths, S., Mitchison, D., Murray, S. B., Mond, J. M., & Bastian, B. B. (2018). How Might Eating Disorders Stigmatization Worsen Eating Disorders Symptom Severity? Evaluation of a Stigma Internalization Model. *International Journal of Eating Disorders 51*, 1010–1014.

Griffiths, S., Mond, J. M., Li, Z., Gunatilake, S., Murray, S. B., Sheffield, J., & Touyz, S. (2015). Self-Stigma of Seeking Treatment and Being Male Predict an Increased Likelihood of Having an Undiagnosed Eating Disorder. *International Journal of Eating Disorders, 48*(6), 775–778.

Griffiths, S., Mond, J. M., Murray, S. B., & Touyz, S. (2014). The Prevalence and Adverse Associations of Stigmatization in People with Eating Disorders. *International Journal of Eating Disorders, 48*(6), 767–774.

Holbrook, T. (2000). Walking in the Woods. In A. E. Andersen, L. Cohn, & T. Holbrook (Eds.), *Making Weight: Men's Conflicts with Food, Weight, Shape & Appearance* (pp. 117–134). Carlsbad, CA: Gürze Books.

Knightsmith, P., Sharpe, H., Breen, O., Treasure, J., & Schmidt, U. (2013). 'My Teacher Saved My Life' Versus 'Teachers Don't Have a Clue': An Online Survey of Pupils' Experiences of Eating Disorders. *Child and Adolescent Mental Health, 19*(2), 131–137.

Kohl, J. (2009). *Skeletal Marriage.* San Jose, CA: CreateSpace.

Laing, R. D. (1960). *The Divided Self: An Existential Study in Sanity and Madness.* London: Penguin UK.

Morgan, J. F. (2008). *The Invisible Man: A Self-Help Guide for Men with Eating Disorders, Compulsive Exercise and Bigorexia*. London: Routledge.
Moss, D. (2012). *Thirteen Ways of Looking at a Man: Psychoanalysis and Masculinity*. London: Routledge.
Norris, M. L., Apsimon, M., Harrison, M., Obeid, N., Buchholz, A., Henderson, K. A., & Spettigue, W. (2012). An Examination of Medical and Psychological Morbidity in Adolescent Males with Eating Disorders. *Eating Behaviors, 20*(5), 405–415.
O'Dea, J. A., & Abraham, S. (2002). Eating and Exercise Disorders in Young College Men. *Journal of American College Health, 50*(6), 273–278.
Oliffe, J. L., Ogrodniczuk, J. S., Bottorff, J. L., Johnson, J. L., & Hoyak, K. (2012). "You Feel Like You Can't Live Anymore": Suicide from the Perspectives of Canadian Men Who Experience Depression. *Social Science & Medicine, 74*(4), 506–514.
Orbach, S. (2005). *Hunger Strike: The Anorectic's Struggle as a Metaphor for Our Age*. London: Karnac Books.
Orbach, S. (2009). *Bodies*. London: Macmillan.
Paterson, A. (2004). *Fit to Die: Men and Eating Disorders*. London: SAGE Publications.
Pirani, B. M., & Varga, I. (2005). The Ethics of Complexity. *Current Sociology, 53*(2), 187–206.
Seidler, V. J. (1989). *Rediscovering Masculinity: Reason, Language and Sexuality*. London: Routledge.
Seidler, V. J. J. (1997). *Man Enough: Embodying Masculinities*. London: SAGE Publications.
Steiner, C., & Perry, P. (1997). *Achieving Emotional Literacy*. London: Bloomsbury Publishing Plc.
Stevenson, C., McNamara, N., & Muldoon, O. (2014). Stigmatised Identity and Service Usage in Disadvantaged Communities: Residents', Community Workers' and Service Providers' Perspectives. *Journal of Community & Applied Social Psychology, 24*(6), 453–466.
Stockford, K., Turner, H., & Cooper, M. (2007). Illness Perception and Its Relationship to Readiness to Change in the Eating Disorders: A Preliminary Investigation. *British Journal of Clinical Psychology, 46*(Pt. 2), 139–154.
Talley, A. E., & Littlefield, A. K. (2014). Pathways between Concealable Stigmatized Identities and Substance Misuse. *Social and Personality Psychology Compass, 8*(10), 569–582.
Vogel, D. L., Heimerdinger-Edwards, S. R., Hammer, J. H., & Hubbard, A. (2011). "Boys Don't Cry": Examination of the Links between Endorsement of Masculine Norms, Self-Stigma, and Help-Seeking Attitudes for Men from Diverse Backgrounds. *Journal of Counseling Psychology, 58*(3), 368–382.

Watson, J., & Nesdale, D. (2012). Rejection Sensitivity, Social Withdrawal, and Loneliness in Young Adults. *Journal of Applied Social Psychology, 42*(8), 1984–2005.

Williams, S. J., & Bendelow, G. A. (1998). *The Lived Body: Sociological Themes, Embodied Issues*. London: Routledge.

Young, S. L. (2012). Personal Stories of "Coming in" and Coming Out of the Closet. *Sexuality & Culture, 16*(2), 205–207.

Young, S., Touyz, S., Meyer, C., Arcelus, J., Rhodes, P., Madden, S., Pike, K., Attia, E., Crosby, R. D., & Hay, P. (2018). Relationships between Compulsive Exercise, Quality of Life, Psychological Distress and Motivation to Change in Adults with Anorexia Nervosa. *Journal of Eating Disorders, 6*(2), 1–8.

Zehr, J. L., Culbert, K. M., Sisk, C. L., & Klump, K. L. (2007). An Association of Early Puberty with Disordered Eating and Anxiety in a Population of Undergraduate Women and Men. *Hormones and Behavior, 52*(4), 427–435.

Zwickert, K., & Rieger, E. (2013). Stigmatizing Attitudes towards Individuals with Anorexia Nervosa: An Investigation of Attribution Theory. *Journal of Eating Disorders, 1*(5), 1–10.

CHAPTER 5

Control and Colonisation

Abstract The man's relationships with his parents is examined against the context of his eating disorder. Former restriction gives way to a loss of control, which overwhelms the man. The self as a battleground with others and the disorder is considered and the eating disorder-as-coloniser of the man's body/self is developed from Campling's work, including the role of power. The foundations are laid for debate between the concepts of gender role conflict and ambivalent masculinities that feature in the book's conclusions.

Keywords Loss-of-control eating • Stigma • Self-as-battleground • Power • Colonisation

The Story of Richard

The memory is not clear about when Richard first consciously decided not to eat but he certainly feels his parents' relationship was the catalyst. Not even being bullied about his weight caused him as much difficulty as his mum leaving his dad. Richard is not the only man with an eating disorder to have highlighted the end of his family unit as being a significant contributory factor and tipping point, as Gareth also experienced this.

R. Delderfield, *Male Eating Disorders*,
https://doi.org/10.1007/978-3-030-02535-9_5

Food Takes a Back-Seat

Despite living with his father following his parents' divorce, his dad became more absent. He was abandoned by his father while his father pursued other relationships. It is not as if his dad simply had a social life, he was gone entire weekends, which seems like a very lonely existence to have as a teenager.

> I can't remember exactly when the first conscious decision to not eat happened but it was shortly after my mum had left my dad. They had an abusive relationship which lasted several years before it exploded when I was fifteen, nothing previously, not even bullying me about my weight had affected me so much. It started with the cooking of meals [...] it was just me and my father left and I took it upon myself to take over the more 'feminine' roles which involved cleaning and more importantly cooking. I disliked the idea of cooking for myself because I never enjoyed the food that I made and I increasingly found that it was easier to eat cereal instead. [...] My dad became more absent [...] and he began his interest in other women ... further afield, which left me on my own ... for weekends at a time.

This implies a connection between the growth of his food issues and being left to fend for himself so much. He ended up feeling like the caregiver in a male-only household and he saw this as adopting a feminised role because he became the housekeeper. Even though he did not like cooking, he did this anyway, making a decision to do the necessary thing even if he derived no pleasure from it (Good and Wood 1995). He did not like his own prepared meals, creating a negative association with food (Keller and Siegrist 2015). He took the option of eating 'easy' food (to spare himself from cooking and to make his life easier) but this meant that it became routine to do that all day, avoiding proper meals.

Richard compensated with dinner money he saved, rather than treating himself to better food or eating out he bought material items, things that he would not have bought otherwise, such as CDs. Given the lack of money in his family, it is perhaps easy to see how this might feel like an attractive option. This meant that lunch was placed as secondary to saving up for 'luxuries'. This makes it less about coveting the luxury items and more about a need to rationalise his food avoidance. Diverting money away from food is not unique to Richard, as Michael (Prager 2010) shares this experience.

People in his family at this point felt that this is where things became out of control but Richard conveys this with a sense of detachment, as if this were their opinion, not his.

> I guess this is where family members would say this is where my actions spiralled out of control, as I would often fill the house with four of five people from Friday through to Sunday, just drinking, playing computer games and watching films. I rarely remember ever making myself food on these days but it was often that the food of choice would be a packet of chocolate biscuits spread out within the weekend.

Control was lost but in a significantly far-reaching way, as he sought to be in company in a rebellious, rather than a nurturing, companionship-seeking, way. Friends stayed all weekend hanging out. Some teenagers would be very happy to have the run of the house for the weekend with their friends. However, for Richard it was a distraction that allowed him to stop thinking about food, firmly side-lining it and even forgetting when he had last eaten (Grilo et al. 2012). When he did eat, it was sparingly, rationing out a packet of chocolate biscuits as his weekend food.

Strange Boy

Later, his care co-ordinator would comment on how strange his behaviours were because of his surviving on a minimal diet of biscuits, yet picking and nibbling at food is quite common in anorexia (Conceicao et al. 2013). Later, he left his dad by choice because the relationship was rocky and Richard wanted to go to college, returning to live at his mum's. Once at his mother's he was forced to go to the doctor's but this did not result in issues with food and eating emerging; rather, his diagnosis was depression.

> Eventually my relationship with my dad broke down in Parallel with my motivation to attend college and I felt I had to move to my mums. It was at this time, aged sixteen, that I was forced to go to the doctors and was diagnosed with depression for the first time. My time at my mums was strange at best, meal times were forced upon me and while with my dad I had absolute control over when I could come in and what I was allowed to do, at my mums there were strict rules that I didn't feel suited me, especially when I was forced to work n evening job at a local factory.

This points to the difficulty clinicians have in diagnosing disordered eating in men (Räisänen and Hunt 2014). Thomas (Holbrook 2000) and Jim (Kohl 2009) were both misdiagnosed, too. Richard was only sixteen when he received this diagnosis, which feels young to have such labels attached. Whether his being forced to get help had a disempowering effect that fuelled his eating issues is not clear. Force is a concept that occurs more than once within Richard's experience, and the issue of force immediately implies concerns about control and personal power.

Richard feels that mealtimes were part of the already strange set-up at his mum's as they were forced on him and he no longer had sole control of his food intake or his weekends, for that matter. This means that the meaning of food changed over time for Richard. His mum used to feed him when his family was intact and this was experienced as nurturing (hence him saying he adopted a similar role for his dad when she left). His dad failed to continue this nurturing in the form of food and mealtimes, and he did not see himself as worthy enough to bother feeding properly. This new regime at his mum's must have been difficult, the fact that after such freedom to come and go as he pleased and restrict his food as much as he did, his food intake was more stringently overseen. Therefore, by the time he was back to eating with his mum, food had lost any connection to nurturing that it might once have had. Another significant life change occurred with the beginning of a new college course but his eating, whilst not having improved, had not worsened either. He was also made to take a job in a factory and ended up moving back in with this dad, whilst trying to study and work. His life choices seemed limited to choosing between neglect or control and little else.

His time at college involved meeting someone and beginning a relationship.

> Towards the latter end of college I began my first serious relationship with a girl from Norwich. Living in Swindon, I found the distance hard and I am pretty sure she found my constant alienation from her frustrating also, as I continuously went through stages of being both nice and then ridiculously horrid to her in equal measure, somewhere along the lines though, she proved herself to me and in what seems to be a blur now, she moved in with me.

Perhaps, the fact that it was a long-distance relationship is not entirely coincidental, especially considering that on top of the geographical distance he also distanced himself from his girlfriend with 'hot and cold' behaviour. This way of relating in relationships is not unique to Richard; other men with eating disorders have made it equally difficult for someone to care about them. Frank (Bruni 2009) pushed away people that he admits wanting to love and Jim (Kohl 2009) repeatedly rebuffed and distanced himself from his wife. It might be that this on-again, off-again behaviour was a test of sorts. She at least experienced both good, as well as bad, with him—enough for her to continue the relationship, and she seemed to pass these trials he put her through.

Dad Becomes a Threat

His memory of the progress of this relationship is indistinct but just as it was becoming serious, and his girlfriend moved in with him, his dad was pulling away again. His dad, in a new romantic relationship, moved out to raise a new family. However, his dad's moving on coincided with a positive change in his food relationship and he gained weight. This demonstrates the distorted nature of an eating disorder: his highest weight (nine stones) was an indicator of better health for him, whereas for me, it was just beyond my lowest weight and represents the mythical ideal for which I purged mercilessly. This evokes feelings of envy that he attained something that I could not achieve.

His dad once again proved to be an unpredictable flashpoint (he seems 'unstable' himself) as he persistently moved in and out of both Richard's and his partner's house. This behaviour has an aggressive, chaotic nature to it. He was threatening to move his new family into the house that Richard had worked hard at redecorating for him and his girlfriend—destabilising his way of life.

> ...the instability of my dad continuously moving to and from the houses, threatening me and my partner continuously that he was going to move in his partner and her children into the house that we had been living in and redecorating for up to a year. The stress from this led to me and my partner splitting up and her moving back to [home].

So, his dad's erratic behaviour contributed to the demise of the three-year relationship (but a positive of this was that Richard eventually went on to meet someone new). In the meantime, however, he was alone again and facing the threat of 'losing' his home as his dad kept to his threat and moved in his new family once he married a new partner. Richard seems to have resented his father seeing the house as rightfully his, when it was Richard and his ex-girlfriend who had paid towards the upkeep and worked on all the improvements. There is a potential question here about how far this sense of injustice contributed to the deterioration of his eating disorder. His father certainly appears to have been very difficult to maintain a relationship with, and by this point he had stopped behaving in any caring, parental way towards Richard just as they should have been transitioning from a parent-child relationship into an adult one.

Richard now felt limited to one room, which must have felt quite painful in a house where he had invested so much of himself and his resources, so he withdrew into darkness, "...very much alone and in hiding" and filled his mind with music (Ahonen 2003: 16).

> ...he was preparing to marry his partner and then move their whole family into what he called ... his house, despite me paying and earning its upkeep. I felt a little trapped and spent much of my time in my bedroom, sitting in the dark, listening to music. From a quiet place, the house turned into a loud atmosphere with the children often screaming at each other [...] which led me to very rarely exit my room ... unless I knew they wouldn't be in. I started to take up ... coastal walks for up to and over six hours a day just so that I wouldn't have to be in the same house...

He really valued the quiet he had formerly had, and this was missed even more when young children creating noise invaded it. The children were naughty and troublesome, and their poor behaviour was not limited to their fighting: everyone in the family suffered from their lack of discipline and Richard suffered from being completely side-lined. Hence, hermit-like, he really did withdraw, yet by this time it was not as if he was a 'moody teenager' wanting to be left alone in his space, he was a young adult. It makes sense that getting outdoors to walk would provide much needed escape from these painful family dynamics. If going for a walk occupied entire days this gives it an excessive edge. Nevertheless, it provided some relief, as it got him out of the situation.

Losing Control

At this point, Richard's food intake really took a hit and became extreme: even basic drinks like cups of tea were disallowed because they contained calories. Hyper-hydration became the norm during the week until Sunday when he had dinner at his mum's and he would have to force himself to eat food, which must have been traumatic.

> My diet literally started to consist of nothing, and I even cut out drinks like tea because I knew the milk contained calories, so for six days a week, I was … living off a large amount of water, with the one day of eating coming on a Sunday when I would be forced to have tea with my mother, which was often a salad. I remember everyone getting worried because we all just stopped talking about food and it would no longer be offered to me, my girlfriend would be called out of the room by her mother, who would 'have words' and she would come back in tears because she couldn't help me.

Although the meal was usually a light one (salad), again there is an idea of coercion being associated with his mum—the family matriarch subjugating the wilfulness of the young male. This appears to be a single element of a diametrically opposed response: his father did not appear to notice (or care) about his food intake or eating patterns at all; whilst his mother did seem to take note, but she expressed this through controlling him. He sensed his family's concern by this time, even though it was not verbalised, rather they changed their behaviours around him. Instead of talking directly to Richard, people asked his girlfriend about his lack of food intake, which greatly distressed her. At home, his family did not talk at all, whilst the other females in his life (his girlfriend and her mother) discussed him without involving him. It is debatable as to whether this would have been the case had the genders been switched: would a man's family have interrogated him about his girlfriend's weight and food habits (Hodges et al. 1998)? Therefore, Richard's girlfriend was made to share responsibility for his condition.

Ultimately, the idea of Richard having a problem with food restriction did not hit home for him until it swung the other way and he began to lose the control that had kept him at such a low weight. Something small would act as a trigger, such as a cautiously chosen 'healthier' food, then it would give way to large amounts of 'unhealthy' food.

> I didn't realise I had a problem until I started binge eating though. I was twenty three years old, I had dropped just below seven and a half stone. The eating of something small like a packet of raisins would turn into cereal and then crisps and then a bar of chocolate and then a bowl of pasta, something very normal for someone to eat in a day would be something I would eat in the space of an hour… I would then feel bloated but most of all, I would feel guilty because I had lost control, this led to me going on longer walks or doing sit ups and press ups just to try and gain control again.

He perceived this as bingeing (Coelho et al. 2013), likening someone's normal intake over the course of a day to what he could speed-eat in a short sitting. This goes beyond hunger and food habits, and is linked to needing to tackle affective states and failing (Lavender and Anderson 2010).

This then had the physical side effect of feeling bloated, which was unpleasant but more importantly for him was the guilt that he felt at the sheer loss of control. Again, the pain and distension of the volume of food coupled with the overwhelming guilt at having behaved this way is a key element in such a cycle (Kelly et al. 2018). This in turn resulted in deliberate exercising-to-compensate to regain the lost control and countermand the binge. After a long delay, some abortive attempts to access professionals who could help followed. Getting help was hampered by anxiety overcoming him and preventing him from keeping the appointments that were arranged. This is not uncommon in men (Griffiths et al. 2015; Räisänen and Hunt 2014).

> It was at this point that I asked for help, six years after originally being referred and after three attempts to even have contact with health professionals because I was often too anxious to go to meetings. The process of recovery is a strange one, physically I have found it fairly easy to feel healthier [...] it is mentally however where the damage I feel has been done. Anorexia and eating disorders in general, seem to affect people in several different ways, maybe this is why they are difficult to treat...

He does not perceive recovery as being straightforward but the physical aspects of it came easy to Richard. This is something that resonates throughout his entire story as he expresses the physicality of what he went through but does not offer as much insight into his emotional state. He acknowledges that he remained under a healthy weight and he definitely conceptualises the bulk of the deleterious effects of his disorder as being more psychological than physical. Richard attributes much of his recovery as being down to a random 'luck-of-the-draw'. Even these days when he is less underweight, shopping for foodstuffs (particularly carbohydrates such as bread) is difficult due to the anxiety it induces.

> I must add, that even now, I find it hard to find employment because of the stigma around the eating disorder because I am a male but most of all, the people who have found it most difficult to deal with and have been most dismissive, have been my family.

His anorexia has affected his professional life and he feels that there is stigma, particularly towards men, which is something that James also asserts. However, this does not compare with the stigma he has experienced from within his own family and how they have slighted him by being cavalier about what he has been through.

Discussion

The Battleground of the Self

In disordered eating the self is often contested ground (Bruni 2012). As previously explored in James's story this is caused by the colonisation of the disorder as it 'sets up home' within the person. Richard's story provides an example of the self as a battleground where war is waged, but war with what or whom becomes the necessary question. The particular area I want to explore with Richard is the idea of gender role conflict, which has some basis in the eating disorders literature (Griffiths et al. 2015c; Murray et al. 2013). Some of Bruch's (1973) early work with women posited something very similar, namely that women developed anorexia as maladaptive way to delay acceptance of the onset of womanhood, their feminine role and their sexuality whilst remaining compliant daughters to their mothers (MacSween 1993). Gender role conflict suggests that men who develop disordered eating or body image concerns do so because they are conflicted about their masculinity; their masculinity has come under challenge or they do not want to fulfil a typically masculine role (Schwartz and Tylka 2008). This suggests the man does not conform to the dominant types of masculinity that are culturally valued; these dominant types are termed hegemonic masculinity (Connell 1995) and operate as a form of 'gender straitjacket' (Pollack 1998) delimiting the ways in which a man can be a man. The concept of hegemonic masculinity warrants further discussion beyond the focus of Richard's story (Chap. 6).

Consistent with this literature, Richard was in an atypical position within his family unit in that he became the homemaker and provider. In particular, he would do the cooking for his father, which is a role traditionally thought to be occupied by a woman and is coded as feminine (Newcombe et al. 2012). He would play host to his friends and allow them to relax, eat and play games, whilst he monitored his intake and denied himself, rationing himself to a few biscuits, again occupying an arguably feminine role (Bordo 2003; Roth 1982). It could be interpreted that Richard struggled with these roles: he did not enjoy being cook and rarely ate what he prepared, instead limiting himself to quick easy food-stuffs that were inconsequential, whilst providing his father with meals. It is also the case that men with anorexia are perceived as being 'feminised' (Griffiths et al. 2013; Murray et al. 2013) or leaning more towards a feminine aspect of themselves, and certainly Richard's relationship with his diet, even counting the calories in cups of tea suggests a more stereotypical feminine approach to food. However, I find this an over-simplistic way of accounting for the struggles that some men have that lead them to anorexia. Suggesting that Richard's relationship with his disordered eating was merely a consequence of conflicts about his gender role fails to consider some of the other aspects of his story as it is presented.

Richard does not share any asperity in his story that would suggest he resented or felt conflicted about being the homemaker during the time he lived with his father, indeed he opted to assume that role. He benefited from an amount of freedom that allowed him great latitude in how he spent his time and money, something that many teenagers would envy. However, with this came a level of alone-ness and, therefore, loneliness as he was left to his own devices whilst growing up. In some ways, Richard's story is the most challenging to interpret as he gives little indication of how he felt or what his motivations were regarding some of his decisions about food. I would suggest that his self was embattled, not by his failure to live up to hegemonic masculine ideals (Knight et al. 2012), but by being set aside and made to feel as if he were secondary and unimportant. The battle within himself was about trying to control that which was beyond him: the affection and attention of a loving family unit.

At this point, the discussion echoes aspects of James's story: the self is social, we develop identities in relation to others around us (Burkitt 2008). Indeed, finding a way to develop and maintain a self-identity through control of the body does not seem so extreme (Chapple and Ziebland 2002) when Richard was left to exist by himself. Later in his story he describes retreating into the dark solitude of his room when he felt under assault from boisterous additions to his family, so even when he was no longer alone, he still had to choose isolation to soothe and protect himself. He felt dismissed by his family and misunderstood by health services, branded an oddity. Moreover, the battle he had with his self and self-control were made starkly obvious when another aspect of his struggle is considered: the breakdown of his carefully controlled inner-world. Despite starving himself through his teenage years, Richard sees beginning bingeing in his twenties as a pivotal point, when he could no longer avoid a sense that things were not alright. Bingeing is a signal that our self-control is no longer to be guaranteed or relied upon. This in turn can lead to the realisation that it is not only our appetites that are running away from us but our emotions, too. It is an alarming and overwhelming experience, when the individual suddenly realises what they are capable of.

Particularly following careful periods of abstinence, as in Richard's case, a binge can be real evidence of the battle within, with part of the self colonised by the disorder, and another part of the self succumbing to a complete loss of control (Campling 2012; Pollert et al. 2013). This signals a "renewed warfare against the appetite and the body" (Chernin 1981: 100). Moreover, binges are "furtive" and take place, generally, in solitude (MacSween 1993). Binges can make the person feel as if there is something fundamentally wrong with them, that they lack all previous control and the inside of a binge is a deep and dark place to be (Roth 1982). This further adds to the isolation that the man experiences. Richard was already quite alone, and must have felt even more so during dark times when he unexpectedly fell prey to bingeing.

The Parent Problem

Richard is the only account in the book whose story is intricately intertwined with that of both parents' behaviours and actions. The broader role of the parents in ensuring balance within the family (Seidler 1997) is important in Richard's story. The way parent's respond to children leads to the development of both self-awareness and awareness of others (Tong et al. 2012), more broadly:

> Our own 'self-feeling' is coloured by the emotional stance that others take, and have taken, towards us ... and some of this stays with us in our reflection on the social world and self. (Burkitt 2012: 471)

Boys feel the sting of divorce acutely (Pollack and Shuster 2000), and his parents' separation came at a time in Richard's life when young people are not as socially embedded as they are as adults (Shiner et al. 2009). Whilst the effects of parents on their children has been explored using female subjects in the eating disorders literature (Bruch 1973; Evans and Legrange 1995; Woodside et al. 2002), what remains unconsidered is this experience in men. Richard is unequivocal about how his family has left him feeling. Rather than providing unconditional love, he feels dismissed and stigmatised.

His absentee father seems to have been more invested in his own social and romantic life than his son's well-being. Had this been the full extent of his relationship with his father this alone would have been enough, as Richard (as discussed above) was left to fend for himself from a young age. This resulted in Richard having to be his own primary carer, cutting short his childhood and impelling him to take on adult responsibilities for himself (Seidler 1997), along with caring responsibility for his father. However, things were much worse. His father's behaviour was selfish and erratic and involved numerous moves in and out of Richard's life as he pursued relationships. This was deeply destabilising. It communicated to Richard his lack of importance. His feelings were disregarded when it came to moving a new family into the house that Richard had cared for and maintained. In essence, Richard had too much freedom as a teenager, left with the run of the house, only to find that as a young adult he went from having an entire house to only his bedroom to escape to.

His mother appears to have been more pro-active in parenting Richard. She set boundaries for him and made him visit the doctor, which is something that had never happened when he lived with his dad. She seemingly 'took over' from his father when things broke down between him and his dad and she provided his home whilst he began to pursue studying. However, this came at a price. Gone was the *laissez-faire* co-habiting that had been the usual state of living at his dad's, where the arrangements were more like room-mates, as there were now rules. Moreover, Richard was made to go out and find work. Later, when Richard had again moved back in with his father, his mother would make sure that he ate when he went over to visit her.

The family is the place that habits are instilled and formed and this is never more so the case than when it comes to food and eating (Atkins and Bowler 2001). Parents, especially mothers, civilise base behaviours around food ensuring the triumph of cultural norms over natural inclinations (Lupton 1996). This is achieved through what is commonly referred to as 'table manners'. Children are schooled from a relatively young age in the propriety of sitting still to eat, using utensils rather than hands, understanding dinner time conventions and conversation. Eating is already an "intensely emotional experience", it soothes, satisfies and satiates but the act of eating is taught as a social practice, something that is shared and that has norms and rules that accompany it (Lupton 1996: 36). This means that whilst eating is an individual, natural requirement, sharing a meal carries a social function (Whitesel 2014). It is a form of communication

(Conner and Armitage 2002) that is passed on from parents, who acculturate children to what are deemed to be acceptable standards of both nutrition and behaviour.

It has also been suggested that "Eating practices in the family are also characterized by struggles over power..." (Lupton 1996: 55), whereby the authority of the parents is challenged through resistance and the exertion of personal choice over family injunctions. The greater the authority of the parents, the more closely aligned will be our food behaviours (Guidetti et al. 2015).

Feeling Forced

Richard was made to do many things that appear in the story: take care of himself, choose between his parents, eat with his mother, give up his house to his father, go to the doctor's, go to work. Richard's story is one of personal disempowerment, having little or no control over key points of his life; this powerlessness is one of the key features of anorexia (Bordo 2003). Any discussion about male power is inevitably set against a backdrop of a Western history of patriarchy and male privilege that continues to this day. However, I approach Richard's experience through the lens of Kimmel (Kimmel and Messner 2010: 159): "Men as a group have power ... but, in their subjective experience of the world, men as individuals do not feel powerful."

Firstly, it is important to establish what I mean here by 'power' in order to understand Richard's powerlessness. This is necessarily brief as I strive to maintain the focus on Richard, rather than examining broader discourses. Power is the capacity to influence and exert authority over oneself, and importantly, others. In eating disorders it can be easy to simplify the idea of power as being the grip the disorder has over the person, and often treatment is about lessening this power and releasing or freeing the individual from entrenched maladaptive habits that have kept them imprisoned (see Bruch 2001), it is a thing that we have or we lack. However, in keeping with Foucault, I would argue that power is not a thing but a relation.

Indeed, it is a multiplicity of force relations and the strategies that these relationships employ (Brod et al. 1996). Current societal expectations rely heavily on self-regulation, as well as social regulation, to order and control individuals (Burkitt 1999). This regulation is as much bodily as it is psychological. Power is "spectral rather than binary": there is more or less of it rather than the absolute of 'power versus no power' (Benatar 2012: 9), which is of importance when we consider Richard's disordered eating. In Richard's story there are multiple interwoven relationships of power, including his relationship with himself. This requires the consideration of two different types of power relations: 'power-over' and 'power-from-within'. Drawing on feminist theory, power-over is synonymous with dominance, coercion and the exercising of authority by one group or person over another. Power-from-within is the power that one exercises over oneself, a form of inner strength that emanates from a sense of our own ability or value (Proctor 2002). As shall be discussed, Richard experiences issues with both.

First and foremost is the relationship, discussed in the section above, with Richard's parents. His father treated him as a person of little consequence, pursuing relationships elsewhere rather than spending time with his son. He conveyed a message to Richard that what he did was of no import to him while, conversely, affording him great personal latitude so that Richard was able to exercise his own choice over how to feed himself and how to spend his time. Therefore, Richard had no control over the relationship with his father, yet complete control over himself. When he met his girlfriend he was even able to home-make with her and take care of the house that his dad was so disinterested in. However, it was not to last. In keeping with the chaotic aspects of his dad's love-life, a new partner and children moved in to Richard's space, displacing him and stripping him of the previous experience of control he had had, as his father reasserted his claim over his home. At best, this was dispiriting, at worst it was debilitating, feeding directly in to Richard's already restrictive relationship with food. He started to live on virtually nothing at all and either retreating to his room or escaping on long coastal walks to get out of the way of his 'new family'.

Before considering Richard's mother, Richard's relationship with his girlfriend is another example which requires attention. In this relationship, he would treat her abysmally, interspersed with better periods. As Richard says, he was "horrid" to her and by his own admission this formed a sort of test that he put her through to ascertain how deeply she felt about him, something which she successfully proved, cementing their relationship. In this way then, despite being powerless to control his home situation, Richard did have power, it was modest and easily lost but it was apparent and he used it to elicit a response from his partner. His girlfriend also became part of another power dynamic between her own family and

Richard, whereby she was questioned 'on his behalf' by her own mother about his behaviour and weight. This had an alienating effect as she was unable to help him and could not provide adequate answers to the questions that were asked, which made her emotional. In a sense, this was disempowering for both Richard and his girlfriend: she would be unsparingly reminded of how little she knew about his inner thoughts and feelings and he was absolved of any reason to give account of himself to someone else, which contributed to providing further space for the disorder to flourish. This has nuances of Josh's experiences, whereby the woman is made the focal point of the man's relationship with food. Here, however, it is not Richard enacting this. Instead there appears to be latent gendered practices being played out in the family, who make his girlfriend responsible-by-proxy, something which is seen in another man's experiences (Hocaoglu 2015).

The penultimate relationship that warrants discussion is that of Richard and his mother. His mother was far more disciplinarian than his father; she imposed her rules on Richard, ones that he found difficult to adjust to, in another example of 'power-over'. Not only was Richard made to go to the doctors but, despite his being in the grip of disordered eating, he was made to go out and work to earn his keep. Food and mealtimes, in particular, can be the site for playing out power within social relationships (Atkins and Bowler 2001), and she forced mealtimes upon him. Even when he did not live with her, she made him join in set mealtimes on a Sunday, although she did not force-feed him huge amounts but prepared salad as the meal. Contrary to the adage that men enjoyed being taken care of through food (Newcombe et al. 2012), Richard perceived eating with his mother as less nurturing and more as an ordeal. There is a danger here of creating a pantomime image of a villainous mother, when there was simply a concerned mum who was trying to take care of his well-being. This said, the interpretation of Richard's experience tuned in to his use of language, including the term 'force' because "women can and do use force and exercise domination over children, over other women, and sometimes over men" (Scott and Morgan 1993: 80). After all, Richard makes it clear that his family became aware that things were not alright with him, yet in his story his mother's response is one of pressure and domination, rather than compassion and understanding.

These two, compassion and understanding, are lacking in Richard's story. He appears to have been misunderstood by everyone around him, even going to the doctor's led to no real understanding. This brings us to the final relationship of power Richard experienced: his relationship with himself, or indeed his lack of 'power-from-within'. There are two elements that I wish to synthesise at this point: the self as battleground and the idea of 'colonisation' (Campling 2012). In previous chapters, I introduced the idea of disordered eating colonising the person, taking him over gradually until he is completely occupied by the disorder. Campling's thesis is that the more the person needs psychic support and sustenance (coping), the more a disordered 'mechanism' can take over core functions of the man and run him for itself. The mechanism, or more fully, the 'defence' mechanism (yet again we find terminology of battle and warfare emerging) does this in order to protect the man from further deterioration of self-worth, and its original goal is laudable: self-preservation and protection. This idea of colonisation is a useful one in framing how a man comes to be in the thrall of disordered eating but there are certain issues with Campling's idea of the mechanism that first need to be addressed.

The mechanism is framed as having an "agenda" and a "function", as being "programmed", all of which sound particularly mechanical. Nevertheless, the mechanism is also theorised as being a "friend" to the man, and the mechanism is capable of experiencing feelings of "well-being" (but only when a much lower weight than is healthy is maintained) (Campling 2012: 8–9). These seem to be very human elements. Campling's theory of the mechanism is, upon analysis, too monadic. In previous chapters, we have encountered the self as social, populated with multiple voices and formed of a constellation of dialoguing aspects of self (Georgaca 2001), rather than there being a single-voiced 'self'. Therefore, the disordered eating is a similarly many voiced, many faceted dialogic phenomenon that pervades the man's thinking, behaviours and habits. It too is populated by the voices of those around us, it has absorbed messages from our environment and attempts to use these to help a man being assailed to cope with the assault. However, as Campling says, it eventually ends up just 'running the show'. It is intimately linked with the issue of self-control and containment as it strives to suppress feelings that are overwhelming (in Richard these would be constantly being dismissed by his father and controlled by his mother, for instance) and replace these with displacement actions, such as restriction and food avoidance. Colonisation remains a useful concept, therefore, because in other meanings, such as anthropology, it is a social concept that involves power, as settlers move in on resources and land, and stake a new claim to a better life, much like disordered eating does.

With this in mind, we can return full circle to the beginning of this discussion about the battleground of the self. Within Richard's story we witness a struggle to be 'himself' in a chaotic disempowering world, where the only way to exercise any power is to isolate himself from the fickle elements around him and control that which is left to him: his body and the food that goes into it. This represents something that begins as power-from-within (the ability to introduce control and nurture for oneself) being swiftly overcome by a form of power-over, where the disorder seizes control of the person. Whilst this is not an inevitable response it is little surprise given the propensity "In western society ... [that] control of the body is seen as fundamental to the maintenance of self-identity." (Chapple and Ziebland 2002: 827). Richard's hungry self had not given up entirely on food, however, and further power struggle is indicated as he battled with himself over bingeing, resulting in guilt and desperate compensation through exercise. Despite modest recovery, his struggles continue.

References

Ahonen, P. S. (2003). *Men's Experience with Eating Disorders: Uncommon Lives? A Look at the Experiences of Men with Eating Disorders.* Chicago: Annual Conference of the American Educational Research Association.

Atkins, P., & Bowler, I. (2001). *Food in Society: Economy, Culture, Geography.* Oxford: Routledge.

Benatar, D. (2012). *The Second Sexism: Discrimination against Men and Boys.* London: John Wiley & Sons.

Bordo, S. (2003). *Unbearable Weight: Feminism, Western Culture, and the Body.* Berkeley, CA: University of California Press.

Brod, H., Callahan, D., Clatterbaugh, K., Grim, P., Gray, J. G., Harris, L., Hopkins, P., LaFollette, H., Laqueur, T., & May, L. (1996). *Rethinking Masculinity: Philosophical Explorations in Light of Feminism.* Lanham, MD: Rowman & Littlefield Publishers.

Bruch, H. (1973). *Eating Disorders: Obesity, Anorexia Nervosa, and the Person Within.* New York: Basic Books.

Bruch, H. (2001). *The Golden Cage: The Enigma of Anorexia Nervosa.* London: Harvard University Press.

Bruni, F. (2009). *Born Round: The Secret History of a Full-Time Eater.* New York: Penguin Press.

Bruni, T. (2012). When the Self Is Contested Ground. *Hastings Center Report, 42*(4), 4–6.

Burkitt, I. (1999). *Bodies of Thought: Embodiment, Identity and Modernity.* London: SAGE Publications.

Burkitt, I. (2008). *Social Selves: Theories of Self and Society.* London: SAGE Publications.

Burkitt, I. (2012). Emotional Reflexivity: Feeling, Emotion and Imagination in Reflexive Dialogues. *Sociology, 46*(3), 458–472.

Campling, M. (2012). *The Nature of Anorexia and Recovery: A Heuristic Self-Search Inquiry.* (pp. 127). London: University of Wales.

Chapple, A., & Ziebland, S. (2002). Prostate Cancer: Embodied Experience and Perceptions of Masculinity. *Sociology of Health & Illness, 24*(6), 820–841.

Chernin, K. (1981). *Obsession, Reflections on the Tyranny of Slenderness.* New York: Harper & Row.

Coelho, J. S., Wilson, S., Winslade, A., Thaler, L., Israel, M., & Steiger, H. (2013). Over-Evaluation of Thoughts About Food: Differences across Eating-Disorder Subtypes and a Preliminary Examination of Treatment Effects. *International Journal of Eating Disorders, 47*(3), 302–309.

Conceicao, E. M., Crosby, R., Mitchell, J. E., Engel, S. G., Wonderlich, S. A., Simonich, H. K., Peterson, C. B., Crow, S. J., & Le Grange, D. (2013). Picking or Nibbling: Frequency and Associated Clinical Features in Bulimia Nervosa, Anorexia Nervosa, and Binge Eating Disorder. *International Journal of Eating Disorders, 46*(8), 815–818.

Connell, R. W. (1995). *Masculinities.* Cambridge: Polity Press.

Conner, M., & Armitage, C. J. (2002). *The Social Psychology of Food.* Buckingham: Open University Press.

Evans, J., & Legrange, D. (1995). Body-Size and Parenting in Eating Disorders—A Comparative-Study of the Attitudes of Mothers towards Their Children. *International Journal of Eating Disorders, 18*(1), 39–48.

Georgaca, E. (2001). Voices of the Self in Psychotherapy: A Qualitative Analysis. *British Journal of Medical Psychology, 74*(2), 223–236.

Good, G. E., & Wood, P. K. (1995). Male Gender Role Conflict, Depression, and Help Seeking: Do College Men Face Double Jeopardy? *Journal of Counseling & Development, 74*(1), 70–75.

Griffiths, S., Mond, J. M., Li, Z., Gunatilake, S., Murray, S. B., Sheffield, J., & Touyz, S. (2015). Self-Stigma of Seeking Treatment and Being Male Predict an Increased Likelihood of Having an Undiagnosed Eating Disorder. *International Journal of Eating Disorders, 48*(6), 775–778.

Griffiths, S., Mond, J. M., Murray, S. B., & Touyz, S. (2013). Young Peoples' Stigmatizing Attitudes and Beliefs About Anorexia Nervosa and Muscle Dysmorphia. *International Journal of Eating Disorders, 47*(2), 189–195.

Griffiths, S., Murray, S. B., & Touyz, S. (2015c). Extending the Masculinity Hypothesis: An Investigation of Gender Role Conformity, Body Dissatisfaction, and Disordered Eating in Young Heterosexual Men. *Psychology of Men & Masculinity, 16*(1), 108–114.

Grilo, C. M., Pagano, M. E., Stout, R. L., Markowitz, J. C., Ansell, E. B., Pinto, A., Zanarini, M. C., Yen, S., & Skodol, A. E. (2012). Stressful Life Events Predict Eating Disorder Relapse Following Remission: Six-Year Prospective Outcomes. *International Journal of Eating Disorders, 45*(2), 185–192.

Guidetti, M., Cavazza, N., & Conner, M. (2015). Social Influence Processes on Adolescents' Food Likes and Consumption: The Role of Parental Authoritativeness and Individual Self-Monitoring. *Journal of Applied Social Psychology, 46*(2), 114–128.

Hocaoglu, C. (2015). Bulimia Nervosa in Males: A Case Report. *The Journal of Psychiatry and Neurological Sciences, 28*(1), 77–83.

Hodges, E. L., Cochrane, C. E., & Brewerton, T. D. (1998). Family Characteristics of Binge-Eating Disorder Patients. *International Journal of Eating Disorders, 23*(2), 145–151.

Holbrook, T. (2000). Walking in the Woods. In A. E. Andersen, L. Cohn, & T. Holbrook (Eds.), *Making Weight: Men's Conflicts with Food, Weight, Shape & Appearance* (pp. 117–134). Carlsbad, CA: Gürze Books.

Keller, C., & Siegrist, M. (2015). Does Personality Influence Eating Styles and Food Choices? Direct and Indirect Effects. *Appetite, 84*(1), 128–138.

Kelly, N. R., Cotter, E., & Guidinger, C. (2018). Men Who Engage in Both Subjective and Objective Binge Eating Have the Highest Psychological and Medical Comorbidities. *Eating Behaviors, 30*, 115–119.

Kimmel, M. S., & Messner, M. A. (2010). *Men's Lives.* Cambridge: Pearson Publishing.

Knight, R., Shoveller, J. A., Oliffe, J. L., Gilbert, M., Frank, B., & Ogilvie, G. (2012). Masculinities, 'Guy Talk' and 'Manning Up': A Discourse Analysis of How Young Men Talk About Sexual Health. *Sociology of Health & Illness, 34*(8), 1246–1261.

Kohl, J. (2009). *Skeletal Marriage.* San Jose, CA: CreateSpace.

Lavender, J. M., & Anderson, D. A. (2010). Contribution of Emotion Regulation Difficulties to Disordered Eating and Body Dissatisfaction in College Men. *International Journal of Eating Disorders, 43*(4), 352–357.

Lupton, D. (1996). *Food, the Body and the Self.* London: SAGE Publications.

MacSween, M. (1993). *Anorexic Bodies: A Feminist and Sociological Perspective on Anorexia Nervosa.* London: Routledge.

Murray, S. B., Rieger, E., Karlov, L., & Touyz, S. W. (2013). Masculinity and Femininity in the Divergence of Male Body Image Concerns. *International Journal of Eating Disorders, 1*(11), 1–8.

Newcombe, M. A., McCarthy, M. B., Cronin, J. M., & McCarthy, S. N. (2012). "Eat Like a Man". A Social Constructionist Analysis of the Role of Food in Men's Lives. *Appetite, 59*(2), 391–398.

Pollack, W. (1998). *Real Boys: Rescuing Our Sons from the Myths of Boyhood.* London: Macmillan.

Pollack, W. S., & Shuster, T. (2000). *Real Boys' Voices*. New York: Penguin.

Pollert, G. A., Engel, S. G., Schreiber-Gregory, D. N., Crosby, R. D., Cao, L., Wonderlich, S. A., Tanofsky-Kraff, M., & Mitchell, J. E. (2013). The Role of Eating and Emotion in Binge Eating Disorder and Loss of Control Eating. *International Journal of Eating Disorders, 46*(3), 233–238.

Prager, M. (2010). *Fat Boy Thin Man*. Los Gatos, CA: Smashwords.

Proctor, G. (2002). *The Dynamics of Power in Counselling and Psychotherapy: Ethics, Politics and Practice*. Monmouth: PCCS Books.

Räisänen, U., & Hunt, K. (2014). The Role of Gendered Constructions of Eating Disorders in Delayed Help-Seeking in Men: A Qualitative Interview Study. *BMJ Open, 4*(4), 1–8.

Roth, G. (1982). *Feeding the Hungry Heart*. Indianapolis, IN: Bobbs-Merrill.

Schwartz, J. P., & Tylka, T. L. (2008). Exploring Entitlement as a Moderator and Mediator of the Relationship between Masculine Gender Role Conflict and Men's Body Esteem. *Psychology of Men & Masculinity, 9*(2), 67–81.

Scott, S., & Morgan, D. (1993). *Body Matters: Essays on the Sociology of the Body*. Hove: Psychology Press.

Seidler, V. J. J. (1997). *Man Enough: Embodying Masculinities*. London: SAGE Publications.

Shiner, M., Scourfield, J., Fincham, B., & Langer, S. (2009). When Things Fall Apart: Gender and Suicide across the Life-Course. *Social Science & Medicine, 69*(5), 738–746.

Tong, L., Shinohara, R., Sugisawa, Y., Tanaka, E., Yato, Y., Yamakawa, N., & Anme, T. (2012). Early Development of Empathy in Toddlers: Effects of Daily Parent-Child Interaction and Home-Rearing Environment. *Journal of Applied Social Psychology, 42*(10), 2457–2478.

Whitesel, J. (2014). *Fat Gay Men: Girth, Mirth, and the Politics of Stigma*. New York: NYU Press.

Woodside, D. B., Bulik, C. M., Halmi, K. A., Fichter, M. M., Kaplan, A., Berrettini, W. H., Strober, M., Treasure, J., Lilenfeld, L., & Klump, K. (2002). Personality, Perfectionism, and Attitudes toward Eating in Parents of Individuals with Eating Disorders. *International Journal of Eating Disorders, 31*(3), 290–299.

CHAPTER 6

Ambivalent Men

Abstract This final chapter gathers emergent conclusions from the interpretative work. Discussion centres around the overarching topics of the title, food, body, and self, with additional focus given to disordered eating masculinities compared with hegemonic masculinity. Relationships with food are configured as sacred or dangerous. Embodiment is examined, debating whether the male eating disordered body can be perceived as a punishing crucible or a fragile artifice. The meaning and significance of fatness for the eating disordered male culminates here. Observations about the reflexive nature of the book are shared and limitations of the study are outlined.

Keywords Male eating disorders • Ambivalent masculinities • Embodiment • Fat • Colonisation • Selfhood

The body "…troubles us. We find that we cannot be at peace in this body that wakes hungering in the morning, filled with urges and appetites we cannot control and are unable to transcend" (Chernin 1981: 56). As men we are no longer immune (if we ever truly were) to the pressures that exert themselves upon us and the regulation of our flesh. Our bodies are the site of triumph and failure. Eating-disordered bodies are home to fractured, divided selves that struggle to maintain a basic level of control in the face of disruption and disintegration. Our selves are temporarily

R. Delderfield, *Male Eating Disorders*,
https://doi.org/10.1007/978-3-030-02535-9_6

protected and then colonised by the disordered eating, we are at once sanctuary and battleground. My aim in this final chapter is to draw conclusions that emerge from the interpretative work.

Food as Sacred and Dangerous (Cregan 2012)

Each man has experienced his own issues around food. The interpretations involved exploring individualised permutations of starving, bingeing, and purging and what these have represented. Despite this, out of the three areas covered by this book (body and self being the remaining two), the concept of food is the one that is the least developed when compared with other stories, where food is heavily discussed and debated (take for example MacSween's (1993) work on female anorexia). Being led by the men's emphasis, my interpretations do not foreground food and eating habits above other aspects of the disordered eating experience, such as relationships with family and others or feelings of low self-worth and fugliness.

For these four men, food is more than nutrition (Kemp et al. 2013; Nash and Phillipov 2014). Consistent with Ahonen's (2003: 3) findings about men, food takes on "massive emotional connotations." More than this, food transgresses the body's boundaries by being taken in and then expelled (Cregan 2012). For a time, as it is digested, it becomes one with us (Schlosser 2012). As Lupton (1996: 16) puts it, by taking in food "we take in the world." Ergo, by refusing to take in food we deny ourselves the world (Gareth, James and Richard) and by overdosing on food we saturate ourselves with what the world has given us and punish ourselves for needing it (Josh, Gareth and Richard). As such, our relationship with food is not a value-free, societally-detached psychological phenomenon. Lupton (1996: 30) also states that there is "a strong relationship between food, emotion and subjectivity" and this is never more so than in the case of disordered eating. What I aim to analyse here are two unifying concepts across the four sets of experiences in terms of the nature of food and its meaning, using Cregan's notion of food as both sacred and dangerous.

The Sacred

Food-as-sacred is evident in each of these men's stories. This means that each man over-values thinking about food and its properties (Coelho et al. 2013), according it status way beyond its nutritional or social function. It becomes totemic, conferred a status that transcends its mundanity (Barthes

2009). Certain foods are favoured and revered. Both Josh and Richard had certain foods that were 'special' to them as their go-to. Focusing on food in these ways allowed the men to experience an escape from aversive affective states (Lavender and Anderson 2010) and the difficult relationships that had caused these.

The links between the (religious) sacred and food restriction have been documented elsewhere (see Hepworth 1999). Here, I want to briefly dwell on the experiences of Gareth and James in restricting their food intake. Gareth went from the ignominy of being a fat young man (discussed further, below) to experiencing the exhilaration of weight-loss and body change. Restricting his food meant that he achieved a much-desired status as a slender man. Having experienced 'the devil in his flesh' (see Chap. 3), his salvation was to throw off the evil of food excess. James attributed benefits and properties to the 'right' food and insisted upon eating only that which he deemed healthful. He moralised about food, and designated it as 'bad' or 'good', as if it transcended its materiality as nutritive fare. In an act of martyrdom, his gruelling approach to restriction allowed him to use abstinence and physical pain to avoid thinking about how imperfect and unlovable he was.

The inverse of food restriction is food excess and there is a kind of sacredness to be found within it. Juxtaposed against Roth's (1982) deep, dark version of a binge, is the immediate ecstasy of emotional numbness and mind-body union encountered in Boskind-Lodahl (1976) or Gregg's (McBride 2014) take on the binge experience. This is far from the furtive, guilt-ridden activity that bingers are routinely reported to engage in Kelly and Carter (2015). It is an escape. It is an all-too-fleeting break from emotional pain and social rejection. It permitted Josh and Richard the chance to be free of difficult feelings, and to experience the sensuality of the food (Bordo 2003) just for that moment. However, bingeing, if left unchecked and uncompensated for, can bring about an ugly body and when food is used in such a way this can be as dangerous as it is restorative.

The Dangerous

Food that might give pleasure and sustenance was experienced as dangerous (MacSween 1993). Our food consumption (or lack of it) communicates messages about who we are and how we feel (Conner and Armitage 2002; Sloan et al. 2010). These four relationships with food communicate significant distress. Sometimes, food itself is to blame for this distress, as we take in too much or too little and regret our decision. For instance, the opposite of the ecstasy of the binge is the guilt and out-of-control-ness felt by Josh and Richard once the food has been ingested. Gareth's food restriction established the possibility of failing his re-invention and James ruined his holiday through debilitating abstinence.

We already know that food is often a response to non-food related issues. An empty self can be filled-up by food as an attempt to deal with the absence of other things (Cushman 1990; Lupton 1996). In Josh's case, he felt the loss of his brother and his family rejection, which led him to the soft comfort food of childhood (Lupton 1996). Gareth had experienced the negative aspects of excess food and the effect this had on him socially, which in turn led to enforced abstinence to remake his body to become someone new (Luciano 2002). James's obsession with healthy eating masked a deep sense of worthlessness experienced in his relationship with his mother and allowed him to maintain distance from others. Finally, Richard restricted his food in response to perceived parental abandonment. These men used food as something it is not: a substitute for belonging and human connection (Bordo 2003) or a solution for disintegrated self-worth.

Lastly, another danger inherent in food is its relationship with gender. Families are known to exert a significant influence on our eating habits and preferences (Guidetti et al. 2015), and men are said to be afforded greater leeway in terms of over-eating; it is less socially-stigmatised (Luciano 2002). Indeed, it may often be encouraged as a sign of masculinity (Bordo 2003). Men have to be "OK with eating anything" (LaMarre and Rice 2015: 12) but their food choices are supposed to confer an idea of "rugged individualism" (Newcombe et al. 2012: 396). As such food is not just nutritive, it can be coded as manly (Whitehead and Barrett 2001) or not.

This is dangerous because it accords a precarious value to food, displacing simple nutrition. Food is linked to how a man should feel about himself and his choices; it contributes to his identity. Yet, here we find men's experiences of willing restriction, a rejection of a manly hearty appetite. These men are *not* OK with eating anything. Food has taken on a different meaning for them, becoming bound-up in their ability to navigate intense emotion and sense of self. When these men over-eat they do not feel socially sanctioned to do so, they feel disgust and distress. Ultimately, however, I leave the final words to Nash and Phillipov (2014: 206), who propose that:

> To date, we still have a limited understanding of the complex ways in which men and masculinities are drawn into the politics, preparation and consumption of food in terms of discursive constructions or embodied experiences.

My work would corroborate this, as food was over-shadowed by other pre-occupations, such as psychological distress and wrecked bodies.

The Eating Disordered Man's Body

Bodies in Western society are under near-constant appraisal (Drummond 2005; Grogan 2016) but whilst "…men's bodies are inserted in a complex web of norms and social relations" (Gill et al. 2005: 56), men themselves do not typically explore the meanings of their own bodies (Brittan 1989; Gough 2018). This said, what we do know is that men's bodies are historical and subjective; they are not just biological processes but storied histories that reveal something about both self and others (Watson 2000). If, as Shilling (2012) suggests, knowledge is grounded in the body, then knowledge can be gleaned about men with disordered eating via their bodies. Whilst I cannot examine all potential 'norms and social relations' that could be brought to bear, I explore two aspects here: firstly, the body as battleground; secondly, the meaning of male fatness.

Punishing Crucible or Fragile Artifice

I return here to a concept raised in Chap. 1 of the male body as a punishing crucible (Gilmore 1994). This punishment is not only psychological, it is meted out on a body that submits and endures it. I challenge Gilmore's statement and suggest that in the case of these men, the body is not just a container for the hot and volatile processes that take place within it (a crucible), it is the ground for entire battles that are waged within and upon it, with both aggressor and victim present.

As men, our bodies are not only objects for the enactment of a separate consciousness, they are our subjective, experiencing points of meeting with the world (Merleau-Ponty 2002). We are constantly engaged with the relationship between our bodily sentience, and the emotions and responses that are encountered as we relate to others. In our relationships, beyond our immediate bodily feelings, are larger messages about the body that envelope and suffuse us. Whilst the body is "…the last remaining seat of individual control over one's own self" (Varga 2005: 229), it is bound up in what society wants it to be, subject to a "tyranny of the Ideal" (Gilmore 1994: 214). Wolf (1990: 187) offers reflection about the female body; however, I have adapted her statement: "…[men's] bodies are not our own but society's." This is at the heart of men's disordered eating, as our body provides the nexus for the assault from others.

Rather than there being a robust, warrior-like, impervious quality (see below) to the bodies featured in these accounts, there is instead a chaos and vulnerability. Josh's body was subject to extremes of violence visited upon him by others. His body was insufficient protection from these assaults; instead, it was the site of great wounding and pain (Törnblom et al. 2015). He, in turn, visited pain upon himself. He attempted to relieve himself of his bodily and psychic experience through suicide. Later, he was to bloat and distend his body, then injure it, with the humiliation and extreme discomfort of laxative abuse. His emotional pain about his body was all too clear, as he felt his fugliness represented a failure to be beautiful, which is a failure to exist successfully (Gilmore 1994).

Gareth's body was acutely socially-situated (Crossley 2001), subject to intense social scrutiny. It caused him great emotional pain, as his fat body was found not just to be wanting but actively repulsive and disgusting. It was so unpleasant to others that it evoked physical reactions of disapproval. His disordered eating was, in part, due to his attempt to reinvent his body, to battle with food and find a slim man within, one that would be sexually attractive and invite arousal rather than aversion. This supports the challenge to ideas that men do not see their bodies as being of "aesthetic interest" (Grogan and Richards 2002: 230). His changing body underwent further mortification when his accident left him wrecked, unable to realise his continued re-invention.

James undertook a battle against his own body (Sanz and Burkitt 2001), beating it into submission with an iron determination that left no crime unpunished (Rohlinger 2002). Food was the enemy and exercise was his weapon to ensure that he was the fittest and healthiest he could be. His body was *the* expression of everything that was wrong with him, the reason why he could not and did not deserve approval, attention and love. If it was not perfect, it was nothing (Bordo 2003). He disavowed his own bodily responses to exertion; he sought separation from the pain of injury and the misery of exhaustion, and used these as proof-positive that he was winning. It took a complete collapse of his ability to function to signal to him that his self-discipline had gone too far, and his own body rebelled against him on holiday.

Finally, Richard used his body as locus of, albeit unstable, self-control and personal retreat. He countered his dad's excesses with his own rationing and restriction, using his body to maintain his sense of identity (Chapple and Ziebland 2002). When he was physically (and emotionally) supplanted by his father's new family, his body was instrumental in his escape plan, drowning out others with music or walking miles. He resisted his mother who tried to control his body through food, work and medicine, yet he exercised his own bodily control that he only truly noticed had existed once a loss-of-control revealed this power-from-within for what it was: a carefully constructed, highly-vulnerable artifice that could not withstand further emotional assaults.

These accounts illustrate a physical expression of a fight-against-and-within-oneself. Here I have artificially separated body and self for the purposes of discussion but in these stories bodies have been the battleground for a war that has been the scourge of a compromised and fragile artifice (Watson 2000). A body that is home to a depleted and colonised self (see below). There is a certain being-in-the-world that the man with disordered eating occupies. His body betrays him, it bends to his will and then, suddenly, it mutinies and rebels against him. In this battle, Connell (2000: 85) says "...the decisive triumph is over oneself and specifically over one's body." Yet, these men are disallowed this triumph. They are subjected to humiliation and pain when their bodies no longer successfully function as a protective, insulating force against life's assailants. Their bodies are too fragile to withstand the onslaught, and they are made to confront their materiality and its disintegration. In disordered eating, men's bodies are not like the medical model where "...the subject is the passive tablet on which the disorder is inscribed" (Bordo 2003: 67). Rather, they are the very place, *le corps propre* (Merleau-Ponty 2002), where disordered eating is lived (Norman 2011).

Escaping Thauvin

I would like to explore a specific example of the body as the site of materiality and struggle. This is important because, to date, no other qualitative study has explored the notion of the meaning of fatness within male disordered eating. Both Josh and Gareth struggled with weight issues. Both were all too aware of the nature of their bodies (Robertson 2006) having been bullied because of appearance and their experiences challenge the literature that suggests men do not experience this as much as women

(Varanese 2013). The fat body, then, has meaning: to be fat means dysfunction and abnormality. It is appetite-out-of-control, troublesome, as stated at the beginning of this chapter. This is graphically illustrated within this treatment of the sport of wrestling:

> Thauvin, a fifty-year-old with an obese and sagging body, whose type of asexual hideousness always inspires feminine nicknames, displays in his flesh the characters of baseness, for his part is to represent what, in the classical concept of the salaud, the 'bastard' (the key-concept of any wrestling-match), appears as organically repugnant. The nausea voluntarily provoked by Thauvin shows therefore a very extended use of signs: not only is ugliness used here in order to signify baseness, but in addition ugliness is wholly gathered into a particularly repulsive quality of matter: the pallid collapse of dead flesh (the public calls Thauvin la barbaque, 'stinking meat'), so that the passionate condemnation of the crowd no longer stems from its judgment, but instead from the very depth of its humours. It will thereafter let itself be frenetically embroiled in an idea of Thauvin which will conform entirely with this physical origin: his actions will perfectly correspond to the essential viscosity of his personage. (Barthes 2009: 5)

This captures a level of public disgust that illustrates the visceral reaction girls had to Gareth's twenty stone frame in his teenage years. As explored in Chap. 3, sexual identity is eclipsed. The fat man may feel sexual, as Gareth did, but this is denied, sensuality and sexuality are stripped away (Gilman 2004), and not expected nor wanted of him (Lupton 2013). There is a cultural norm at play that suggests that the addition of muscle is not enough: it is the absence of fat that will restore the man's sexuality (Peterson and Anderson 2012) and right to positive regard. To be thought of as 'stinking meat' evokes an image of foul-smelling lifeless flesh past-its-best in a butcher's shop, a sight that engenders deep disgust and nausea, not wild passion.

In Josh's story, being fat is bad enough but, as shown by Thauvin, fat *is* ugly: they are one-and-the-same. Fat is "both devoured and devours the body…" (Gilman 2004: 9). The transgressive act of food intake (see above) can transform the body into something to be scorned and reviled (Orbach 2009). It takes over the body and makes it malformed and offensive to behold. Fugliness means a complete debasement, the fugly man is common and worthy of condemnation. He is not well, not functioning, not whole (Monaghan 2007) and is deemed grotesque (Scott and Morgan 1993). He cannot escape his body. It is immediately visible (Monaghan 2005). He wears it like a flesh-prison, the clothes barely containing what lies beneath. Even if there is no obvious disdain or degradation to be found, he perceives it everywhere and nowhere is safe. The fugly body is not a reliable or wholesome place to live from. Its equation with dysfunction and sickness means the man is constantly judged as an individual failure (Orbach 2009) in a society that revels in wealthy abundance of food but perversely venerates those who resist.

This failure is perceived as an emasculation (Monaghan 2007), it is "unmanly" (Gilman 2004: 9). Therefore, fat is linked to defective forms of masculinity (Bell and McNaughton 2007). Once again, masculinity appears, this time linked to bodies rather than food. A fat man is a non-man, a spoilt man (Lupton 2013; Temple Newhook et al. 2015). Masculinity is challenged through ideas of what 'looks' attractive, this is the lookism at work that we encountered earlier. These men strove to escape the stigma and social disapprobation that their fatness engenders. The nature of this stigma is unlike others, it has a "master status" because it exercises such control over the body and the responses it evokes (Whitesel 2014: 31). They no longer wanted to arouse the judgment, malevolence and revulsion of the people around them (Reece et al. 2015), and so they had to change their relationship with their bodies. Disordered eating took hold within this context: one of being socially abused and sexually negated all because of our abiding obsession with fat (Greenhalgh 2012).

The Self in Jeopardy

The self is not a single unitary phenomenon. Earlier in the book, I argued that the self is socially-voiced, composed of the people and messages that have influenced us since birth. Human beings are not contained psychological units with a single accountable self. In other qualitative research, the idea of self is under-explored and although the self is alluded to Ahonen (2003), it remains analysed as a psychological function alone. I have divided the discussion here into three concepts separated into two parts; however, it is important to note that the distinction has been made purely for the sake of clarity. Experientially, these three aspects are interwoven and form part of an even greater complexity of selves that can be found in works such as Burkitt (2008) and Eakin (1999). Despite the idea of social selves, for ease of expression I explicitly refer to 'self' in the singular when describing moments of experiencing the self, rather than 'selves', even though I have made the point that we are plural in nature. I am not striving for a theory of selfhood, merely to illuminate some of the ways these interpretations demonstrate aspects of our selves as men with disordered eating.

Stigmatised Selves

It has been suggested that men feel stigma more acutely than women (Wilkins and Kemple 2011). Stigma is not only the result of a spoiled identity (Goffman 1963), it actively creates one. Doyle and Molix (2014) report that stigma erodes relations by corrupting our self-image to the point that our ability to be in relationship with someone else is significantly impaired. This is because it leads to excessive self-protection and results in the establishment of barriers to protect our identity. This can be seen in Richard's interpretation where it is the stigma felt from his own family that is the most injurious to him. In this way, most of Richard's disordered eating behaviours can be seen as congruent with protecting himself from further disregard and neglect.

Stigma arises in the research literature, particularly relating to men accessing treatment. This is evidenced in James, where he feared stigma at work, should he disclose his disorder to his employer. This links to selfhood since James could not risk ruining the one aspect of himself that afforded him an unspoilt and successful identity: his professional life. The corrupting effects of stigma are such that the self needs only fear its potential to seek to avoid it. As discussed in Chap. 4, stigma is a social curse. To feel it is to expose oneself to the world and its judgement and derision. We are made to feel "not quite human" (Goffman 1963: 14). However, there is more to this. Help-seeking has been coded as feminine (Oliffe et al. 2012; Vogel et al. 2011), and, as can be seen in other qualitative research on males (Räisänen and Hunt 2014), men fear 'having a woman's problem'. Therefore, the integrity of the man's self is assaulted twice: first, to be eating-disordered is feminine; second, to ask for help is, well, even more feminine. Once again, the concept of what is masculine (in this case as the opposite of feminine) emerges as an issue within disordered eating (more about this below).

Another aspect of stigmatised identity that is coded as feminine is that of fat. The bodily and social aspects of fat men are discussed above but the fat man is not just bodily spoiled. His selfhood is implicated. There are direct associations between the individual and public perceptions of his ability to regulate and govern a self that is seen to be out-of-control and failing. The fat body is an "abomination" of the self (Goffman 1963: 14). It is a visible communication to those around us that we do not conform to societal expectations about how to manage emotions, appetites and impulses. Gareth and Josh were not just perceived as unappealing aesthetically, they were also seen to be vile, weak people who deserved mistreatment. This is echoed elsewhere, where people (especially those with visible symptoms, such as underweight in anorexia and overweight in binge-eating disorder) were felt to be at fault (Austen and Griffiths 2018; McLean et al. 2014). These are selves that are fundamentally flawed. They have succumbed to their own caprice and it is perceived that they have only themselves to blame for their damaged identities. To be an eating disordered man is to be culpable and deserving of (public) reproach.

Divided and Colonised Selves

In James's story, I alighted on some of Laing's work about a divided self. I want to return to this here. In Josh's interpretation, the extreme hardship he experienced left him struggling to cope with loss, violence and rejection, hating himself in the process. Gareth suffered loneliness and overt rejection by his peer group, living as an object of revulsion. Richard made his girlfriend 'prove' that she cared for him, as he subjected her to a pendulum of behaviour: pushing her away then showing he wanted her. These men are caught in a dilemma. On one hand, they want to be noticed and their existence validated "...in order to maintain [a] sense of realness and identity. Yet, at the same time, the other represents a threat to [their] identity and reality" (Laing 1960: 113). The self, and not just the body, is experienced (unwantedly) as 'fragile' (Giddens 1991).

This fragility evolves because men are dependent on interaction with others to 'truly' experience themselves. In turn, this leaves us vulnerable to dislike, disapproval, and rejection. These negative messages become part of our internal storying about ourselves (Eakin 1999) because they form part of the multiplicity of selves that populate us. Therefore, the notion of a divided self is somewhat misleading. This is more than the self being simply 'divided' by these conflicting experiences of others (Burkitt and Sullivan 2009). Rather, this can be viewed using Laing's idea (proposed in Chap. 4) of a 'dissolution into non-being'. A complete ontological disintegration begins to make sense, not just as discussed for James, but for all four men. All have had their experience of 'being' under attack. Their experience of being valued men was contingent upon the positive appreciation of others, and this is something they did not receive in a way that met their needs. This argument is strengthened by Giddens (1991) discussion of Laing's work. Not only do these damaging life experiences and fragmented personal relationships lead to an ontologically insecure self, they lead to a retreat (Pollack 1998) from life into narrow, protective forms of coping.

In this coping the self becomes "disembodied" (Giddens 1991: 59). This disembodiment is a rupture between self and the lived experience of the body. A man may feel detached from experiencing the body as desirable (for example, Josh's fugliness or Gareth's wanting to feel attraction). The man may be able to withstand physical 'attack' more so than others can (for instance, Josh's endurance of bodily violence and James's punishing exercise regime and starvation). Becoming disembodied allows the man to find safety ontologically, detached from his defective, rejected or assaulted physicality (for example, Richard's eschewing proper food for long walks away from the unsafe step-family environment) (Giddens 1991). The self is given over to the voice of the other(s), it sits in judgment, evaluating from a distance (Burkitt 1999), the body becomes an "...instrument manipulated by the self from behind the scenes" (Giddens 1991: 59).

By this time, the self is fragile, damaged and in danger of disintegrating, and it is at this point that the disordered eating can successfully step in as 'caretaker'. At first, it 'visits' to take care of the man, to run things 'behind the scenes' and manage his self, holding it together by making sense of the others' voices, rationalising them and finding the body wanting and in need of improvement. It settles in the territory that is vacated by the remnants of ontological security and offers the man a way of being that is more manageable. It colonises the man's self and sets about restoring control amidst chaos and pain (Campling 2012). The body is relegated to a fleshy project that can be used for punishment, reward or self-improvement through the careful regulation or comforting injection of food.

A facsimile of ontological security is experienced as real because, initially at least, the external pressures are soothed and allayed as long as certain behaviours and bodily and emotional responses are routinely experienced. As with most attempts at colonisation, elements of self that resist are wiped out and brought under the auspices of the new governance. Rebellion may actively be staged but it is met with a brutal dose of punishment and recrimination. The body becomes the terrain that is changed and moulded by the coloniser for its own purposes. The daily human need of food becomes the primary focus for the coloniser who wants to make sure the body responds to the will of the self, the body must represent the extensive work performed by the man on his self (Allen 2008). A focus on food and, perhaps, exercise or purging behaviours also ensures that the colonised terrain is all-too-aware of its boundaries using its business of daily living to maintain this focus and avoid the jeopardy of aversive emotional states (Kristeller et al. 2006). A temporary respite from a dreaded complete ontological disintegration is thus achieved.

Where Is the Fighting, Fucking and Football? (Mac an Ghaill 1994)

The idea of what it means to be a man has arisen in one form or another throughout the previous chapters. We encountered: a challenging of the stoic male stereotype and of the assumption that men prefer a muscular body; the idea of passing as a 'normal' man'; and the problem of the male experience of personal power. Now I would like to create a contrast. Firstly, I examine the topic of masculinity from findings that have emerged from studying men and their well-being. Then I explore the four accounts in light of these propositions.

Hegemonic Masculinity and the Buff Agenda

The literature analysed in Chap. 1 belies some assumptions that formed part of my thinking when formulating my interpretations. For instance, current research features the impact of a pursuit of muscularity on male eating disorders. Another theme from the reviewed studies was that of Gender Role Conflict where gender is said to be "...social practice that constantly refers to bodies and what bodies do" (Connell 1995: 71). These ideas both rely heavily on a conceptualisation of male gender as a particular form of masculinity.

Hegemonic masculinity is used to denote the dominant form of how to be a man, constructing manhood as a social phenomenon and giving an account of masculinity that is "culturally exalted" (Connell 2000: 84). To function it must have role models that society can refer to as being the ascendant ideals of 'being a man'. There are certain features of hegemonic masculinity that concern us here. This form of masculinity requires compulsory heterosexuality, it repudiates the feminine (Seidler 1997) and the effeminate (Kimmel and Messner 2010), it is bound up in power relations, it involves bodily mastery and control (Connell 2000), including remaining 'silent' (Coates 2008), and imperviousness is a must. The man is a provider and is financially independent, a so-called 'bread-winner'. The epitome of manhood must always be willing to engage in violence when necessary. He should have sex with women and should be known for doing so. He should identify with masculine displays of skill, camaraderie and sportsmanship, like that which is found on a football pitch (Mac an Ghaill 1994).

The latest addition to the arsenal of a 'real man' is a body that is resolutely not feminine. To be lean, strong and fit is no longer enough: a hyper-muscular body is said to be essential (Murray and Touyz 2012). The man must look every bit as overtly strong and tough as he should feel. His masculinity is as unassailable as his 'stylish hard body' (Alexander 2003). This challenges older ideas that the male body is merely instrumental, that the body is for action rather than aesthetic (Seidler 1997). This hegemonic masculinity knows that what is on display on the outside is a projection of oneself on the inside (Gill et al. 2005). Failure to be as attractive as possible implies a complete failure as a man (Gilmore 1994). In addition, there is a masculine relationship with food: a man can eat whatever he wants but should never let it show on his body; his body must be his project, taut and toned and definitely not fat. This is the 'buff' agenda (Siconolfi et al. 2009), the duty of the man to be as sculpted and defined as he can. The buff body is implicated heavily in sexuality (McCabe and McGreevy 2011), and "no pecs, no sex" is its mantra (Bordo 2003: xxiii). To be buff is to be beyond reproach, the man's masculinity is not in question. He may spend his days working in finance, using soft skills and sitting at a desk but he is a warrior at heart and has the body to match: the brain of a banker, the body of warrior.

Throughout this chapter I have referred to 'masculinity' as if it were exactly what is described above. However, hegemonic masculinity is not without its shortcomings. For instance, it has been argued that more young men are turning away from an "unattainable ideal of masculinity" (Kimmel 2008: 42) and instead are opting to live in a protracted form of adolescence, where responsibility and settling into manhood are eschewed in favour of spending time with friends and a single lifestyle, contradicting the idea of the man as the 'bread-winner'. The notion of hegemonic masculinity is also challengeable on the grounds that it does not adequately take account of the idea of masculinities, in the plural. This view suggests that at any one time there is more than one way to attain status as an ideal man within society (Anderson and McCormack 2014). Coupled with this is the postulation that masculinity itself is a fragile (Mac an Ghaill 1994; Segal 2007) and enigmatic construct (Garlick 2003). This means that presenting masculinity as a dominant, objective pattern of ideal 'maleness' is highly questionable as men themselves struggle to articulate what it means (Moller 2007). Instead of embracing an ideal of manhood with gusto, many men experience reticence about leaving boyhood and becoming 'real men' (Wilkins and Kemple 2011) and often report the opposite of what hegemonic masculinity represents [see Pollack's work (1998) for detailed examples of this].

Disordered Eating Masculinities

Into this discussion enter the four sets of experiences explored in this book. It could be argued that not one of these men present an explicitly expressed affiliation to so-called dominant forms of masculinity. Even James, who pursues the allegedly (new) masculine practices of health and fitness (Crawshaw 2007), prefers solitary exercise to male-bonding team sports. Likewise, Gareth, who wants to feel attractive to women, does not present himself as wanting to fulfil the manly ideal of Mac an Ghaill's (1994: 56) "fucking" so much as meeting a companion who will desire and want him, following so much rejection. None of the men reflect specifically on their manhood, which is interesting given the assertion that "Gender is perhaps the most fundamental determinant of an individual's sense of self." (Wilkins and Kemple 2011: 112). Instead, masculine gender can be gleaned by what emerges from their experiences with self, their bodies, and with others, but there is little overt evidence of these men struggling to attain an ideal of masculinity. Josh, Gareth, James and Richard appear to give credence to the observation that "For many men their gender ... remains unseen if not incomprehensible to them." (Whitehead 2002: 81). This suggests that the experience of being a man is an unconscious one that operates beyond the immediate awareness of the individual man.

However, this is misleading because, in line with the masculinity theory above, the men encounter various gendered experiences, for example, in terms of power and self-control. Josh has power-over exerted upon him in the form of violence, whilst Richard struggles with power-from-within as he loses control of his carefully managed aloneness. They also experience their sexuality as men. Josh and Richard maintain relationships with the opposite sex, and Gareth is actively aware of what he perceives women will find attractive, whilst James recognises his expectation to fail as a boyfriend and distances himself from potential girlfriends. James also aspires to a successful role as a worker and takes great pride in his ability to be seen to function well in his professional life, which is consistent with another feature of supposed hegemonic masculinity.

In the act of telling their story, these men do not appear to worry about appearing as less than a manly guy. Nor do they disguise the trauma they have endured, the pain they have experienced nor how ugly and damaged they have felt. What the accounts evidence is a significant amount of gender ambivalence. Rather than supporting an idea of a dominant form of masculinity, these four stories seem to be more consistent with a non-culturally ascendant take on masculinity (Hanlon 2012). Just as eating disorders in women may suggest an ambivalence about culturally validated feminine norms (Orbach 2006), so too does disordered eating in men suggest a gender ambivalence when it comes to societal ideals of masculinity. Instead what we are exposed to are less stereotypical forms of being a man (Peterson and Anderson 2012). These men show their desire for belonging and an awareness of the anxiety involved in vulnerability (Pollack 1998). Gareth, for instance, wanted a body that represented a youth he had never really had. Also, they want connection. Take, for example, Richard's thwarted desire to enjoy a domestic life with his girlfriend or Gareth's yearning for acceptance from other boys only to find they were self-interested and cruel, resulting in him fostering virtual friendships online, where he holds concurrently contradictory-yet-non-distressing feelings about his use of pro-Ana spaces in the regulation of his bodily practices.

This gender ambivalence is a unique aspect of this research and signifies an internal battle that each man faced. It highlights that these four men struggled with issues of being themselves and living in their own skin first and foremost. They found their identities under assault from the world in which they lived. The eating disorder's colonisation came about through ontological insecurity to which each man responded differently. Josh struggled with his worth as an individual based on his looks. Gareth sought a non-hegemonic way of fulfilling his desire to be attractive, through slenderness not muscle. James struggled with being the perfect son and boyfriend but strove for perfection in his body management through exercise, and Richard found himself the unabashed home-maker for an unappreciative, neglectful father. In some ways, Josh and Richard were victims of hegemonic ideals: Josh found himself subject to another man's violence and Richard was abandoned as his father responded to divorce by pursuing girlfriends.

This suggests that disordered eating masculinities, in the case of these stories, are multiple, complex and punctuated with confusion and contradiction about being a functioning, coping man who is immune to assaults on the self. This challenges the somewhat simplistic take on manhood presented in previous research (see Chap. 1), where the eating disordered male was said to be a sensitive 'feminine' person. In one way, their disordered eating was a 'typically male' stoic attempt to self-manage all alone; in another way, they challenge masculine stereotypes by coming forward and sharing their stories, breaking the silence that is said to typify men (Kimmel 2008).

These men also demonstrated ambivalence about gendered roles and practices. Gareth sought to be a slim, boyish man not dissimilar to the 'girlish' women he wanted to attract, and freely admits this. Richard codes certain roles as 'feminine' but this is stated without disapprobation or intrapersonal conflict. The roles being associated with feminine practices are not thusly diminished. Indeed, keeping his reduced family unit functioning in the absence of a female caregiver, appears as a key element of his experience. He goes on to be a homemaker when settling in the house with his girlfriend. This holds value for him, as evidenced by his responses when this home-building is undermined by his father's actions. The idea of gender ambivalence is subtler and more nuanced than Gender Role Conflict. GRC suggests an internal struggle against a unitary idea of masculine gender, whereas gender ambivalence allows for the influence of external relations and forces on a man's experience and expectations of masculinity. There is fluctuation and indecision along with, at times, an embracing of non-stereotypical experiences of being a man, in the absence of both an internal gender struggle or a need to justify practices as 'manly'.

This is contrary to the masculine-hyper-vigilant manner observed in recent work with men about gendered (bodily) practices. Taking the example of health and aesthetics, such as weight-loss, grooming or cosmetics (Gough 2018), men seemingly cannot help but justify their practices using reasoning immanent to hegemonic masculinities, where action and heterosexuality are core. This involves framing cosmetic use as being practicality not vanity, for example make-up is not about beauty but about a practical response to health issues (redness due to a skin complaint). 'My girlfriend does it, I should show her the same respect'-type statements are evident when it comes to personal care and grooming or invoking 'what women want'. For instance, shaping or eradicating body hair is related to being more sexually appealing to the opposite sex. Gareth's experiences about like-attracting-like are indicated here.

Ultimately, with ambivalence, what the men experience is better described as 'contradictions', rather than 'conflicts', whereby the man has mixed feelings about gendered experiences, holding contradictory ideas that co-exist simultaneously. This ambivalence is run through with both internalised and externalised ideas of manhood but with a dose of practical personal meaning-making, where the man is not judging himself in binary terms: masculine or feminine, manly or not.

The Personal in the Professional

I am not devoid of similar experiences to those discussed above. One of the advantages of an interpretative approach, and one of the oft-unreported aspects of male eating disorders research, is the reflexive element. I have fiercely worked to keep this reflexivity present in the book. These stories, along with the other accounts I studied, have had a profound effect upon me personally. They enriched and enlarged my understanding of both the phenomenon of eating disorders and my own relationship my disordered eating. The stories have also changed my understanding of what it means to be a man. I have let go of earlier feelings of isolation and feel a great sense of relief. Therefore, I have benefited as much personally, as I have professionally, from working with these experiences.

It should be noted that despite sharing my own story as the backdrop to this research, I did not return explicitly to my story, nor did I subject it to analysis. This is a shortcoming of the work in this book. However, my personal experience continued to emerge throughout the analysis and its impact on the finished interpretations requires brief consideration. The decision to open with my story yet leave it un-analysed was a difficult one but it was done to achieve an honest transparency without it dominating, so that focus could remain on the contributed experiences.

Like all qualitative work, there is a personal investment from the researcher. At the beginning, I resolutely assured my doctoral supervisors of how prepared I was to study men's experiences as a fellow experiencer. My constant companion, my research journal, demonstrates how wrong I was. The emotional labour involved was immense. I am glad I spent some time on my personal response to the stories, as I was to return to these throughout. Interpretative work involves multiple readings, living with texts for days and weeks, and searching through other parallel texts to support an interpretation. Sometimes, I found it so painful to be constantly with a story, as I interpreted and reinterpreted it, that I had to put it aside and take a break. I certainly found that "In dealing with the body and the emotions we are dealing with [is] that which is closest to us, as researchers ... with our very sense of the being in the world" (Scott and Morgan 1993: 19). As can be seen in interpretations and discussions, some of my personal response survived until the 'final' version of the interpretation. These tend to represent some of the times I connected so thoroughly with an experience that it felt painful and reassuring all at once. Often, I found talking to trusted others would re-ground me and allow for empathy rather than emotional contagion to take hold. However, when this was not enough, I engaged in counselling at different points of the process to deal with residual pains of my own that the interpretative work was revealing.

At different points I was surprised by own emotional response that, at first encounter, could have prevented me from remaining with a text and interpreting it as faithfully as possible. Gareth's pro-Ana experiences were so challenging at the time that some of the issues became part of his chapter. This really illustrated to me how inculcated I had become with medical discourses around how bad these spaces were for users, yet Gareth's experience was far more complex than a simple good/bad binary. In James's story I found a fellowship because the first phase of my disordered eating involved significant amounts of excessive exercise: I had to deal with overwhelming feelings of nostalgia. Richard's story evoked envy, I seethed with it early on in the process. He was able to attain a weight of nine stones 'easily', whereas for years I struggled bingeing, purging and exercising and only got as low as nine-and-a-half stones. I had to find ways to move beyond these potential impasses with the text and congruence was the solution.

On a final personal note, Bell and McNaughton (2007) suggested that it is not good to study men in isolation. I disagree strongly with this assertion. Feminist work has made no apologies for placing women at the heart of its endeavours, and rightly so. When it comes to mental health disorders that affect mind, body and self we need more work by men, about men, for men. This will help address the aetiolation identified by Jones and Morgan (2010) at the beginning of this book and begin to combat the lack of men's voices in eating disorder research (Gill et al. 2005). I have benefited significantly from the extensive feminist eating disorders literature. In the future I hope that researchers will be able to draw on a rich male-generated literature, too.

Conclusion

There is a single way to capture all future possible research recommendations, which is to state that any one of my propositions within the previous chapters could be subjected to further study. This is the nature of exploratory research, after all, to begin conversations rather than to offer resolute answers. This book is the beginning of a longer body of interpretative work, not the completion of a finite exegesis. Social and cultural interpretation is always incomplete and there is no final word to be had (Bordo 1999). This incompleteness is evident in the limitations of this book. Key aspects of the human experience fail to make an appearance. I have been unable to offer any analyses on class, race or disability, for example. My analysis is also restricted to that which can be gleaned from disembodied texts (the irony of which, given the focus on embodiment, is not lost on me). I have striven to be as comprehensive as possible but the act of interpretation is subjective and inferential; access to a different collection of texts would understandably yield different insights.

A limitation of note is that which appears in the first chapter, then seemingly vanishes throughout the rest of the book. I am referring to media as a pertinent socio-cultural phenomenon. It has been postulated that there is a growth of normative discontent among men, that generalised body dissatisfaction is no longer limited to the experience of women (Tantleff-Dunn et al. 2011). The media is suggested as one of the reasons for this growth in bodily discontent, particularly among males (Doumit et al. 2018; Wright et al. 2016). Although my instinct is that media is likely implicated, as its impact is analysed in other research (Jankowski et al. 2011), not one of my contributors alluded to it. Having left the men to decide what they would write in their stories, I have to respect that that there is no attention given to this phenomenon.

Notwithstanding such limitations, the interpretations in this volume suggest that Bordo's (2003: xx) assertion about women may hold true for some men's experience: "The 'profile' of [people] with eating problems is dynamic, not static, heterogenous, not uniform." The research presented here has offered original insights and has tried to remain faithful to its aim of exploring experiences of disordered eating. I would like to end with a particular emphasis, which has emerged through engagement with the stories and has been presented as a strand throughout this final chapter. The "drip, drip, drip of the … perfect male" continues (Jankowski et al. 2011: 7) and I would propose that more men in the West may succumb to its vice-like grip. Men's understanding of the embodiment and experience of their own masculinities is critical to addressing the potential harm that this may cause.

In the realm of disordered eating and body image, we need more work on men. They have been under-represented and the balance needs to be redressed, as the effects of society and culture on men may become more dangerous to their health (Gill et al. 2005). Men themselves would benefit from recognising more diversity among them, from embracing a multitude of ways to be a man. Operating within strict binaries of how to live our gender is as damaging for men as it is for women (Hanlon 2012). We need to raise our young men to reach out for the connection and relationships they need, and to recognise that self-worth is equally as important for both genders. These four stories show the terrible physical and psychological pain men have endured to be in the world. At times, this pain has been due to the colonising effects of the disordered eating; yet worse, at other times, this has been meted out by others around them. As men, our social context, our gender and our disordered eating are inextricably woven together and our attempts to understand the meaning of these are only just beginning.

References

Ahonen, P. S. (2003). *Men's Experience with Eating Disorders: Uncommon Lives? A Look at the Experiences of Men with Eating Disorders.* Chicago: Annual Conference of the American Educational Research Association.

Alexander, S. M. (2003). Stylish Hard Bodies: Branded Masculinity in Men's Health Magazine. *Sociological Perspectives, 46*(4), 535–554.

Allen, J. T. (2008). The Spectacularization of the Anorexic Subject Position. *Current Sociology, 56*(4), 587–603.

Anderson, E., & McCormack, M. (2014). Cuddling and Spooning Heteromasculinity and Homosocial Tactility among Student-Athletes. *Men and Masculinities, 18*(2), 214–230.

Austen, E., & Griffiths, S. (2018). Why Do Men Stigmatize Individuals with Eating Disorders More Than Women? Experimental Evidence That Sex Differences in Conformity to Gender Norms, Not Biological Sex, Drive Eating Disorders' Stigmatization. *Eating Disorders*, 1–24. DOI: 10.1080/10640266.2018.1499337.

Barthes, R. (2009). *Mythologies.* New York: Hill and Wang.

Bell, K., & McNaughton, D. (2007). Feminism and the Invisible Fat Man. *Body & Society, 13*(1), 107–131.

Bordo, S. (1999). *The Male Body.* New York: Farrar, Straus and Giroux.

Bordo, S. (2003). *Unbearable Weight: Feminism, Western Culture, and the Body.* Berkeley, CA: University of California Press.

Boskind-Lodahl, M. (1976). Cinderella's Stepsisters: A Feminist Perspective on Anorexia Nervosa and Bulimia. *Signs, 2*(2), 342–356.

Brittan, A. (1989). *Masculinity and Power.* Oxford: Basil Blackwell.

Burkitt, I. (1999). *Bodies of Thought: Embodiment, Identity and Modernity.* London: SAGE Publications.

Burkitt, I. (2008). *Social Selves: Theories of Self and Society.* London: SAGE Publications.

Burkitt, I., & Sullivan, P. (2009). Embodied Ideas and Divided Selves: Revisiting Laing Via Bakhtin. *British Journal of Social Psychology, 48*(3), 563–577.
Campling, M. (2012). *The Nature of Anorexia and Recovery: A Heuristic Self-Search Inquiry.* (pp. 127). London: University of Wales.
Chapple, A., & Ziebland, S. (2002). Prostate Cancer: Embodied Experience and Perceptions of Masculinity. *Sociology of Health & Illness, 24*(6), 820–841.
Chernin, K. (1981). *Obsession, Reflections on the Tyranny of Slenderness.* New York: Harper & Row.
Coates, J. (2008). *Men Talk.* Chichester: John Wiley & Sons.
Coelho, J. S., Wilson, S., Winslade, A., Thaler, L., Israel, M., & Steiger, H. (2013). Over-Evaluation of Thoughts About Food: Differences across Eating-Disorder Subtypes and a Preliminary Examination of Treatment Effects. *International Journal of Eating Disorders, 47*(3), 302–309.
Connell, R. W. (1995). *Masculinities.* Cambridge: Polity Press.
Connell, R. W. (2000). *The Men and the Boys.* Cambridge: Polity Press.
Conner, M., & Armitage, C. J. (2002). *The Social Psychology of Food.* Buckingham: Open University Press.
Crawshaw, P. (2007). Governing the Healthy Male Citizen: Men, Masculinity and Popular Health in Men's Health Magazine. *Social Science & Medicine, 65*(8), 1606–1618.
Cregan, K. (2012). *Key Concepts in Body and Society.* London: SAGE Publications.
Crossley, N. (2001). *The Social Body: Habit, Identity and Desire.* London: SAGE.
Cushman, P. (1990). Why the Self Is Empty: Toward a Historically Situated Psychology. *American Psychologist, 45*(5), 599–611.
Doumit, R., Kharma, J. A., Sanchez-Ruiz, M., & Zeeni, N. (2018). Predictors of Disordered Eating in Young Males. *Community Mental Health Journal, 54*(2), 236–244.
Doyle, D. M., & Molix, L. (2014). How Does Stigma Spoil Relationships? Evidence That Perceived Discrimination Harms Romantic Relationship Quality through Impaired Self-Image. *Journal of Applied Social Psychology, 44*(9), 600–610.
Drummond, M. J. N. (2005). Men's Bodies: Listening to the Voices of Young Gay Men. *Men and Masculinities, 7*(3), 270–290.
Eakin, P. J. (1999). *How Our Lives Become Stories: Making Selves.* New York: Cornell University Press.
Garlick, S. (2003). What Is a Man?: Heterosexuality and the Technology of Masculinity. *Men and Masculinities, 6*(2), 156–172.
Giddens, A. (1991). *Modernity and Self-Identity: Self and Society in the Late Modern Age.* Cambridge: Polity Press.
Gill, R., Henwood, K., & McLean, C. (2005). Body Projects and the Regulation of Normative Masculinity. *Body & Society, 11*(1), 37–62.

Gilman, S. L. (2004). *Fat Boys: A Slim Book*. Lincoln, NE: University of Nebraska Press.

Gilmore, D. D. (1994). The Beauty of the Beast: Male Body Imagery in Anthropological Perspective. In M. G. Winkler & L. B. Cole (Eds.), *The Good Body: Asceticism in Contemporary Culture* (pp. 191–214). Oxford: Berghahn Books.

Goffman, E. (1963). *Stigma: Notes on the Management of Spoiled Identity*. London: Simon and Schuster.

Gough, B. (2018). *Contemporary Masculinities: Embodiment, Emotion and Wellbeing*. Cham, Switzerland: Springer.

Greenhalgh, S. (2012). Weighty Subjects: The Biopolitics of the U.S. War on Fat. *American Ethnologist, 39*(3), 471–487.

Grogan, S. (2016). *Body Image: Understanding Body Dissatisfaction in Men, Women and Children*. London: Routledge.

Grogan, S., & Richards, H. (2002). Body Image: Focus Groups with Boys and Men. *Men and Masculinities, 4*(3), 219–232.

Guidetti, M., Cavazza, N., & Conner, M. (2015). Social Influence Processes on Adolescents' Food Likes and Consumption: The Role of Parental Authoritativeness and Individual Self-Monitoring. *Journal of Applied Social Psychology, 46*(2), 114–128.

Hanlon, N. (2012). *Masculinities, Care and Equality: Identity and Nurture in Men's Lives*. London: Palgrave Macmillan.

Hepworth, J. (1999). *The Social Construction of Anorexia Nervosa*. London: SAGE Publications.

Jankowski, G., Diedrichs, P. C., & Halliwell, E. (2011). *Men and Body Talk*. Bristol: University of the West of England.

Jones, W. R., & Morgan, J. F. (2010). Eating Disorders in Men: A Review of the Literature. *Journal of Public Mental Health, 9*(2), 23–31.

Kelly, A. C., & Carter, J. C. (2015). Self-Compassion Training for Binge Eating Disorder: A Pilot Randomized Controlled Trial. *Psychology and Psychotherapy: Theory, Research and Practice, 88*(3), 285–303.

Kemp, E., Bui, M., & Grier, S. (2013). When Food Is More than Nutrition: Understanding Emotional Eating and Overconsumption. *Journal of Consumer Behaviour, 12*(3), 204–213.

Kimmel, M. S. (2008). *Guyland: The Perilous World Where Boys Become Men*. London: Harper New York.

Kimmel, M. S., & Messner, M. A. (2010). *Men's Lives*. Cambridge: Pearson Publishing.

Kristeller, J. L., Baer, R. A., & Quillian-Wolever, R. (2006). Mindfulness-Based Approaches to Eating Disorders. In R. A. Baer (Ed.), *Mindfulness-Based Treatment Approaches: Clinician's Guide to Evidence Base and Applications* (pp. 75–91). Burlington, MA: Academic Press.

Laing, R. D. (1960). *The Divided Self: An Existential Study in Sanity and Madness.* London: Penguin UK.
LaMarre, A., & Rice, C. (2015). Normal Eating Is Counter-Cultural: Embodied Experiences of Eating Disorder Recovery. *Journal of Community & Applied Social Psychology, 26*(2), 136–149.
Lavender, J. M., & Anderson, D. A. (2010). Contribution of Emotion Regulation Difficulties to Disordered Eating and Body Dissatisfaction in College Men. *International Journal of Eating Disorders, 43*(4), 352–357.
Luciano, L. (2002). *Looking Good: Male Body Image in Modern America.* London: Macmillan.
Lupton, D. (1996). *Food, the Body and the Self.* London: SAGE Publications.
Lupton, D. (2013). *Fat.* Abingdon: Routledge.
Mac an Ghaill, M. (1994). *The Making of Men: Masculinities, Sexualities and Schooling.* London: McGraw-Hill Education UK.
MacSween, M. (1993). *Anorexic Bodies: A Feminist and Sociological Perspective on Anorexia Nervosa.* London: Routledge.
McBride, G. (2014). *Weightless: My Life as a Fat Man and How I Escaped.* New York: Central Recovery Press, LLC.
McCabe, M. P., & McGreevy, S. J. (2011). Role of Media and Peers on Body Change Strategies among Adult Men: Is Body Size Important? *European Eating Disorders Review, 19*(5), 438–446.
McLean, S. A., Paxton, S. J., Massey, R., Hay, P. J., Mond, J. M., & Rodgers, B. (2014). Stigmatizing Attitudes and Beliefs About Bulimia Nervosa: Gender, Age, Education and Income Variability in a Community Sample. *International Journal of Eating Disorders, 47*(4), 353–361.
Merleau-Ponty, M. (2002). *Phenomenology of Perception.* London: Routledge Classics.
Moller, M. (2007). Exploiting Patterns: A Critique of Hegemonic Masculinity. *Journal of Gender Studies, 16*(3), 263–276.
Monaghan, L. F. (2005). Big Handsome Men, Bears and Others: Virtual Constructions of 'Fat Male Embodiment'. *Body & Society, 11*(2), 81–111.
Monaghan, L. F. (2007). Body Mass Index, Masculinities and Moral Worth: Men's Critical Understandings of 'Appropriate' Weight-for-Height. *Sociology of Health & Illness, 29*(4), 584–609.
Murray, S. B., & Touyz, S. W. (2012). Masculinity, Femininity and Male Body Image: A Recipe for Future Research. *International Journal of Men's Health, 11*(3), 227–239.
Nash, M., & Phillipov, M. (2014). Introduction to the Special Issue: Eating Like a 'Man': Food and the Performance and Regulation of Masculinities. *Women's Studies International Forum, 44*(1), 205–208.
Newcombe, M. A., McCarthy, M. B., Cronin, J. M., & McCarthy, S. N. (2012). "Eat Like a Man". A Social Constructionist Analysis of the Role of Food in Men's Lives. *Appetite, 59*(2), 391–398.

Norman, M. E. (2011). Embodying the Double-Bind of Masculinity: Young Men and Discourses of Normalcy, Health, Heterosexuality, and Individualism. *Men and Masculinities, 14*(4), 430–449.
Oliffe, J. L., Ogrodniczuk, J. S., Bottorff, J. L., Johnson, J. L., & Hoyak, K. (2012). "You Feel Like You Can't Live Anymore": Suicide from the Perspectives of Canadian Men Who Experience Depression. *Social Science & Medicine, 74*(4), 506–514.
Orbach, S. (2006). *Fat Is a Feminist Issue*. London: Arrow Books.
Orbach, S. (2009). *Bodies*. London: Macmillan.
Peterson, G. T., & Anderson, E. (2012). The Performance of Softer Masculinities on the University Dance Floor. *The Journal of Men's Studies, 20*(1), 3–15.
Pollack, W. (1998). *Real Boys: Rescuing Our Sons from the Myths of Boyhood*. London: Macmillan.
Räisänen, U., & Hunt, K. (2014). The Role of Gendered Constructions of Eating Disorders in Delayed Help-Seeking in Men: A Qualitative Interview Study. *BMJ Open, 4*(4), 1–8.
Reece, L. J., Bissell, P., & Copeland, R. J. (2015). 'I Just Don't Want to Get Bullied Anymore, Then I Can Lead a Normal Life'; Insights into Life as an Obese Adolescent and Their Views on Obesity Treatment. *Health Expectations, 19*(4), 897–907.
Robertson, S. (2006). "I've Been Like a Coiled Spring This Last Week": Embodied Masculinity and Health. *Sociology of Health & Illness, 28*(4), 433–456.
Rohlinger, D. A. (2002). Eroticizing Men: Cultural Influences on Advertising and Male Objectification. *Sex Roles, 46*(3–4), 61–74.
Roth, G. (1982). *Feeding the Hungry Heart*. Indianapolis, IN: Bobbs-Merrill.
Sanz, J., & Burkitt, I. (2001, April). Embodiment, Lived Experience and Anorexia: The Contribution of Phenomenology to a Critical Therapeutic Approach. *Athenea Digital, 0*, 38–52. Retrieved from https://nbn-resolving.org/urn:nbn:de:0168-ssoar-64373.
Schlosser, E. (2012). *Fast Food Nation: The Dark Side of the All-American Meal*. Boston, MA: Houghton Mifflin Harcourt.
Scott, S., & Morgan, D. (1993). *Body Matters: Essays on the Sociology of the Body*. Hove: Psychology Press.
Segal, L. (2007). *Slow Motion: Changing Masculinities, Changing Men*. Basingstoke: Palgrave Macmillan.
Seidler, V. J. J. (1997). *Man Enough: Embodying Masculinities*. London: SAGE Publications.
Shilling, C. (2012). *The Body and Social Theory*. London: SAGE Publishing.
Siconolfi, D., Halkitis, P. N., Allomong, T. W., & Burton, C. L. (2009). Body Dissatisfaction and Eating Disorders in a Sample of Gay and Bisexual Men. *International Journal of Men's Health, 8*(3), 254–264.
Sloan, C., Gough, B., & Conner, M. (2010). Healthy Masculinities? How Ostensibly Healthy Men Talk About Lifestyle, Health and Gender. *Psychology and Health, 25*(7), 783–803.

Tantleff-Dunn, S., Barnes, R. D., & Larose, J. G. (2011). It's Not Just a "Woman Thing:" the Current State of Normative Discontent. *Eating Disorders, 19*(5), 392–402.

Temple Newhook, J., Gregory, D., & Twells, L. (2015). 'Fat Girls' and 'Big Guys': Gendered Meanings of Weight Loss Surgery. *Sociology of Health & Illness, 37*(5), 653–667.

Törnblom, A. W., Werbart, A., & Rydelius, P.-A. (2015). Shame and Gender Differences in Paths to Youth Suicide Parents' Perspective. *Qualitative Health Research, 25*(8), 1099–1116.

Varanese, J. (2013). Social Construction of Deviance: Male Body Image. *Sociological Imagination, 2*(1), 1–13.

Varga, I. (2005). The Body—The New Sacred? The Body in Hypermodernity. *Current Sociology, 53*(2), 209–235.

Vogel, D. L., Heimerdinger-Edwards, S. R., Hammer, J. H., & Hubbard, A. (2011). "Boys Don't Cry": Examination of the Links between Endorsement of Masculine Norms, Self-Stigma, and Help-Seeking Attitudes for Men from Diverse Backgrounds. *Journal of Counseling Psychology, 58*(3), 368–382.

Watson, J. (2000). *Male Bodies: Health, Culture and Identity*. Buckingham: Open University Press.

Whitehead, S., & Barrett, F. J. (2001). *The Masculinities Reader*. Oxford: Polity.

Whitehead, S. M. (2002). *Men and Masculinities: Key Themes and New Directions*. Cambridge: Polity.

Whitesel, J. (2014). *Fat Gay Men: Girth, Mirth, and the Politics of Stigma*. New York: NYU Press.

Wilkins, D., & Kemple, M. (2011). *Delivering Male: Effective Practice in Male Mental Health*. London: Men's Health Forum.

Wolf, N. (1990). *The Beauty Myth: How Images of Beauty Are Used against Women*. London: Random House.

Wright, J., Halse, C., & Levy, G. (2016). Preteen Boys, Body Image, and Eating Disorders. *Men and Masculinities, 19*(1), 3–21.

Index

R. Delderfield, *Male Eating Disorders*,
https://doi.org/10.1007/978-3-030-02535-9